Career Questions?

Ask *Angela*

A JOB-SEEKER'S GUIDE
TO FINDING THE PERFECT JOB!

Angela I. Schutz

STERLING PUBLISHING GROUP

Career Questions? Ask Angela
- A Job-Seekers Guide To Finding The Perfect Job

Published by The Sterling Publishing Group, USA 1.888.689.1130
www.SterlingPublishingGroup.com

Printed in the United States of America

Cover and book design by Jodi Nicholson www.JodiNicholson.com
Edited by Jodi Nicholson of SPG www.SterlingPublishingGroup.com

This book may be ordered through the publisher or by contacting:
Angela I. Schutz, 554 Boston Post Road, Suite 171, Orange, CT 06477
Email: a.schutz@driventosucceed.net   www.driventosucceed.net

ISBN: 978-0-9845010-7-6
Education & Reference: Career | Guides | Interviewing | Job Advice

This book is dedicated to my parents,
Louis and Marion Iovieno,
who taught me the importance of being
a strong woman and thinking for myself.

Although they are no longer with me,
I feel their presence every time
I work to move my life forward.

I miss them every day and am eternally
grateful for their unconditional love.

Praise for Angela Schutz and

Ask *Angela*

"Angela Schutz is an outstanding individual and a true professional! I had the opportunity and pleasure to work with her when I lost my position in the recent downsizing. She was my outplacement advisor and career counselor, and successfully helped me through the transition process and navigate the rough economic waters to locate and land a great position! I can't say enough good things about her. She is a great person and I would I highly recommend her!"

- Carmen D.

"Angela is a highly respected professional in the career development and counseling field. She is very knowledgeable, motivated, and a trusted source for excellent advice and guidance. Angela is extremely dedicated and fully commits her time and resources to her clients' needs to ensure successful outcomes."

- Kathy P.

"This little gem of a book is packed with great insights and innovative ideas to help you land the job of your dreams. Entertaining, informative and engaging, this book will give you practical advice on how to have the kind of attitude that will make a positive impact on the way to find your next position."

- Jack Canfield
Co-author of Chicken Soup for the Soul® series

"Angela and I had the opportunity to work together for a number of years on a professional association's Professional Development committee. Together, we managed two programs, one in Hartford and one just outside of Boston. Angela was a dedicated member of the committee who worked hard to ensure the programs were successful. Angela went above and beyond the call of duty when she researched and presented a workshop to colleagues on professional social networking sites when they were in their infancy. Her presentation was clear, well researched and presented. Angela then led a very thoughtful dialogue with her peers about the merits and pitfalls of these sites. Angela is a very competent professional who does what she says when she says it will be done. I look forward to working with Angela again on other committees."

- Robbin B., Director
Roger Williams University

"If you are looking for a practical job-finding toolkit all in one book, you have found it in Ask Angela: A Job-Seeker's Guide to Finding the Perfect Job! Angela has a direct, no-nonsense approach to finding employment that will both inspire job-seekers and give them practical get-off-your-butt action items. I especially like the question and answer sections that are chock full of information every job-seeker should know. She covers all aspects of finding employment from resumes to salary negation and even the in's and out's of using social media sites such as Linked In®. If you or someone you know is looking for a new job, I highly recommend reading Ask Angela!"

- Donna Kozik
MyBigBusinessCard.com

Praise for Angela Schutz and Ask Angela

"Angela is one of a handful of influential people in my life. I unexpectedly lost my employment over a year ago and had the fortune to get out-placement assistance from Angela Schutz. This happened during a time when, skills or no skills, there were less and less jobs. The normal channels of gaining employment where drying up and my industry was in a holding pattern. Angela's can-do attitude was invaluable. She would repeat the same message: The jobs are out there, you just have to find them. This message was backed up with actual skill to accomplish the task, always keeping up with the latest solutions to fit the ever challenging problem of selling oneself. Not being in sales, a lot of this was new to me. Interviews became an enjoyable human interaction instead of a dreaded afternoon. I think it was the caring that made the real difference. Angela's continual concern that you keep your self-worth high and a balance with the rest of your life is the quality that really helped during a job search. I now have the ideal job that Angela said was there. Thank you Angela."

- Raymond E.

For a complimentary copy of

Ask *Angela's* INTERVIEW TIPS

Visit www.driventosucceed.net

Career Questions?

Ask *Angela*

A JOB-SEEKER'S GUIDE
TO FINDING THE PERFECT JOB!

Angela I. Schutz

STERLING PUBLISHING GROUP

Foreward

Over the past decade I have met literally hundreds of career coaches and resume critiquers ever since I founded Women For Hire, a company that hosts career expos for women across the country.

They volunteer at our events to help job-seekers. By and large they're a good bunch of people with decent motives who help others during one of the most stressful times any of us can have: when we're out of work.

Angela Schutz, who has critiqued many a resume for us and spoken at many of our expos, stands out from the rest. I admire her dedication to her craft of helping people from all walks of life during their career transition. She takes herself and her work very seriously – and has invested extensively in training to arm herself with the best knowledge to serve her clients. I've watched her at work – compassionate, and always focused on delivering great results. Angela knows her craft – and she knows it well.

Although this little book is just a little over 100 pages, Angela gets right down to it. Isn't that what everyone needs today? No nonsense. No fluff. Just results. Whether it's determining your path, writing an effective resume, acing an interview or figuring out what kind of salary to ask for, it's all here—and so much more. Angela doesn't disappoint.

Tory Johnson
CEO, Women For Hire

Acknowledgments

In Gratitude

Over the years, I have coached many job-seekers and their questions have led me to put together this guide. The inspiration for the guide came from the weekly networking team meetings that I facilitated. Every week, I was amazed by the questions that were asked. And so, just as every new idea is formed from a kernel of knowledge, the idea came to me that most job-seekers have questions and very often, there is no one to answer them. This guide is meant to answer those questions and help you start a productive and exciting job search. It is my hope that you will understand, after reading this book, that although there are tools to facilitate the job search process, the most important thing you can do is enjoy the search and revel in the gifts and strengths that make you unique. In the end, it is your uniqueness that is attractive to new employers.

Special thanks go out to Teams 1 and 2 who have motivated me to move forward on this project. My deepest, everlasting gratitude goes out to my mentors: Jack Canfield, Co-Author of the Chicken Soup for the Soul® series and author of The Success Principles; Marcia Wieder, Founder of Dream Coach University®; Tory Johnson, CEO and Founder of Women for Hire and Spark and Hustle; Donna Kozik, www.mybigbusinesscard.com and Write a Book in a Weekend; and Robert MacPhee, author of Manifesting for Non-Gurus. All of whom have inspired and encouraged me to stand in my purpose, dream big dreams, manifest great results, and live life with "Spark and Hustle".

My admiration goes out to MJ Paris for her passion and positive inspiration, Sean Smith who is wise beyond his years and has truly motivated me, and Don Helton, whose support is invaluable.

Special thanks go out to my coaches, Michelle Woolard Pippin www.womenwhowow.com and Jodi Nicholson, Founder of Success Coach Institute and www.JodiNicholson.com who have served as my GPS's in the business world. They mean business about growing a business and have each been a delight to work with, all butt-kicking aside!

I was blessed to be raised by loving, generous parents who knew the meaning of family, hard work and giving back to the community. My father was the strong, silent type who gave me the gift of understanding non-verbal communication – a true gift. My mother was equally strong and a fabulous role model for women of all ages. From the time I was a very young girl, she blessed me with her own form of leadership training: Be the engine, not the caboose.

My unending love and gratitude go out to my son, Peter, whose creative genius has brought this book to life, and without whom life would be meaningless for me. He is my heart!

Last, but in no way least, I am deeply grateful for the love of friends I have made over the years. The support of a good friend is like nothing else on earth! Each friend is like a precious jewel, worthy of care and admiration. I have been amply blessed with precious friends who have stood by me, even when they were scratching their heads wondering what I would do next! I have many friends who have stuck with me for more than thirty years and whether seasoned friends or new, I cherish each and every one of them for all the joy they have brought to my life.

For those of you with a "fire in your belly" to do something more in your life, I strongly encourage you to find a mentor who will guide you to develop the strengths with which you were born.

Dare yourself to dream big, and then, dare yourself to follow that dream. What a beautiful world we live in where dreamers can dream, and create and learn and grow and make a difference!

If you are reading this book because you are looking for a job, just trust that the right job is out there for you, and it will find you. Have fun meeting all sorts of new people on this journey. Give yourself permission to enjoy the process, because it can be a truly amazing ride!

~Angela

Table of Contents

Introduction

This book is written for all those job-seekers who feel there are no jobs out there. It is my intention to demystify the process of finding a good job in a reasonable length of time, and more importantly, empower you to step into your own skin and own your skills and talents. If there is one message I hope you garner from reading this book, it is that your uniqueness is the most significant part of the job search process. Once you understand that no one will ever be able to do a job exactly the way you would because you are a combination of your cultural influences, your innate talents and the skills you have amassed along with your unique combination of personality traits. No one has ever been you and no one can ever be you, so take some time before you begin your job search to reflect on the elements that make you exactly who you are today.

Appreciate how far you have come in your life and develop all of your innate talents so that you can be the best "you" possible. Taking the time to know who you are will help you develop some confidence, and there is nothing more attractive to a new Hiring Manager than to be able to hire a new employee who has the education, skills and talents needed to step into the posted position, and can do it with confidence. Use the time in which you are job-hunting to get organized. Do some of the things that bring you happiness, and especially the things that you often find yourself complaining you had no time to do while you were working.

Another element to look at is the "you" that you present to the world. Are you up to date in your "look"? Do you sport a modern hairstyle? Is your clothing current rather than out dated? Are you up to date with your technology skills? While you have some extra time now that you are unemployed, you can use some of the time to learn more computer skills so that when you return to work, you are ready to face any new computer challenge presented to you.

Lastly, looking for a new job can feel like a lonely activity. It doesn't need to be. There are networking groups, job search work teams, your state labor board and Career Coaches out there who will support you during your search, and applaud you when you land your next job. Don't spend every day alone when there is so much help out there.

I wish you great success, and would love to hear about your progress! I hope this book will give you a practical guide for finding that new job, and for finding the best "you" within you.

Let the journey begin!

1 Chapter One

How To Get Started

"If you follow the crowd, you will likely get no further than the crowd. If you walk alone, you're likely to end up in places no one has ever been before. Being an achiever is not without its difficulties, for peculiarity breeds contempt. The unfortunate thing about being ahead of your time is that when people finally realize you were right, they'll simply say it was obvious to everyone all along. You have two choices in life. You can dissolve into the main stream, or you can choose to become an achiever and be distinct. To be distinct, you must be different. To be different, you must strive to be what no else but you can be." — Unknown

The process of finding a new job that supports who you are has never been an easy one, but with the economic downturn in 2008, incredible hurdles in the job search process were created. That being said, you need to approach the task of finding a new job, just as you would any new project at work – plan the work and work the plan.

It is not uncommon for a job-seeker who has recently been severed from their former organization to experience a host of feelings such as anger, grief, rage, depression and even elation. It is important to recognize those feelings and be realistic about them. If you are feeling any form of anger, you need to kick those feelings to the curb and realize that the person, or organization that laid you off can't hurt you anymore. In fact, they don't even know that you are angry. Moreover, every time you bring them into the conversation, it is as if they have their hands around your throat! In reality, you are in complete control and can alleviate some of the anger by simply not talking about them. Your time would be better spent by practicing a script that will allow you to speak comfortably about who you are professionally and what your demonstrated strengths or areas of expertise are.

If you are an introvert, or have always had trouble extolling your strengths, it will definitely take some practice to be comfortable talking about your professional expertise. You need to find words that won't make you feel as if you are bragging about yourself. You may say something like, "I've had some successes in the areas of…" and highlight the things that have gone well in your career. Find the words that speak to your strengths yet allow you to be comfortable. When you are on an interview, your ability to speak to your strengths is a key element in landing the job. Like most forms of exercise, it gets easier with practice. Keep practicing until you are comfortable. You just can't wiggle out of talking about the strengths and abilities you possess for the job to which you are applying, and expect the Hiring Manager to know s/he should hire you.

Your feelings are real, and if you are taking more than two or three weeks to get over feeling of anger or grief, seek help. Find someone who will listen to you and help you deal with those feelings. Find a trusted friend or a professional counselor. It is best to only talk with one person about how ridiculous you feel that the company was to let go of someone as great as you. Remember, no matter how tempting it may be, never chose a confidant who is in any way connected to your former employer. Information regarding someone's inability to cope with a lay off seems to travel with lightning speed.

Many years ago I heard an expression that has served me well over the years: "Keep your words sweet, you may have to eat a lot of them"! Seriously, if your feelings are a problem, get help, but the bottom line is that the sooner you move into a more positive approach to finding your next position, the better off you will be, and the sooner you will get to experience the honeymoon phase and elation that comes with having a new position that taps into your professional strengths. There is nothing better than working for an organization that wants you and is excited about what you can do for them!

The element that you need to keep in the forefront of your search is productivity. Your productivity is, and needs to be, measured every day. This is a simple act that will make an incredible difference in your life, so treat it as such.

Set daily goals for yourself. Each goal needs to be in the format: how much by when? Make the goals measurable. For example, it is better to say: I will make five networking calls each day for the next five days than to say I will increase my network this week. With measurable goals, both you, and anyone you choose, can actually measure your success. On Friday you have either made twenty-five calls or you haven't. By using this method, success becomes easy to measure and celebrate. Please don't forget to celebrate the small successes along the way. It will prove to be of tremendous value as you move forward toward landing your next job.

Your success is very much determined by your willingness to approach your search for a job in a different way from the way you have been told to conduct it in the past. Contrary to the belief of most job-seekers, the process of finding a job needs to be extremely proactive. You need to structure each day by creating an action plan and sticking to it.

There is no room for broken resolutions here! Schedule your day to include physical exercise, face-to-face networking with others, sending out applications, following up with former colleagues or hiring managers with whom you have already spoken, internet time, and time to engage in activities that nourish your spirit, such as spending time with family and friends.

Yes, taking time, each and every day, to feel good about yourself and your life is important. It will help keep you from becoming depressed.

Besides, the few months that you will be out of work are a gift. You now have the time to do some of the things you complained about not having time to do when you were working 60 hours per week. You will soon be back on the "hamster wheel", so allow yourself to enjoy some of this free time to reconnect with family, friends, and YOURSELF.

Although you may have suffered from "workaholism" in the past, don't allow yourself to fall into an intense state of " job-seekerism"! Keep your job search and your life in balance. You do not need to spend forty hours per week looking for a job. The two things you absolutely need to do is spend some quality time everyday networking with others and you need to be positive about who you are and what you have to offer your next employer.

Another potential pitfall of the job-seeker is to fall into a passive job search. We are often deluded by the thought that we are "looking for a job" when we spend endless hours surfing job boards or when we give our resumes to recruiters. You should not be simply handing over your resume to just any recruiter and expect high-level results. Nor should you passively sit in front of your computer hour after hour pouring through the listings on the infinite number of job boards that currently exist.

Your ultimate success will be determined by your productivity. Never let a day go by where you haven't interacted with people. It is much easier to take part in passive activities that delude us into thinking we are looking for a job, but don't be fooled. Networking is the way to accelerate your job search so that you land the job of your dreams in the least amount of time.

Whenever you are networking, introduce yourself professionally, highlight your areas of expertise and a particular strength you have that makes you unique, and tell what level you have achieved. Your clarity will shorten your job search, provided that you spend some part of every day interacting with people – adult people. Spending time with your kids doesn't count toward looking for a job unless you are networking with other parents at your child's soccer game or swimming lessons. Why, you might ask? It is because statistically, the way you will get your next job will be through networking.

I love statistics, and the most recent statistics that have come across my desk are that only one in eighteen hundred people gets a job from a job board, while one in eight people gets a job through networking.

Unfortunately, most people get lured into spending 85% of their time on the computer surfing the job boards. It makes little sense. The rate of return is dismal, but the computer is extremely seductive. You think you should check out the newest job listings and before you know it, five hours have passed! You then feel the need to rationalize that you have spent five hours looking for a job, but in reality you have wasted most of that time.

There are two things I know about job-seekers, most do not live with anyone who has a new job for them, and most believe that the jobs they see posted on the job boards are real. Neither of these ideas is helpful in your pursuit of new employment. Turn off your computers, get out of your houses and start talking with others. Brainstorm with everyone.

When you put all of your energy and belief into job boards, you are often sadly disillusioned. Most of you have worked at companies that have decided to promote from within, yet they post the job externally.

Poor you! You are surfing the job boards and find the job that seems to have your name all over it. You spend hours writing a great cover letter and meticulously scanning your resume for errors so that your application submission will be perfect. You spend weeks waiting for a reply and the potential interview offer. Unfortunately, the company will never see your application because they plan to promote from within.

Get moving, there are always jobs out there, but you need to make the commitment to spend each and every day networking with others to uncover those hidden, but oh, so real jobs.

Lastly, I need to make a plug for Career Coaches. There are so many benefits for you when you enlist the services of a coach. One of the beauties of the coaching relationship is that a coach will allow you to dream your dreams and never tell you that you weren't good at the thing you desire to do. Usually coaches leave those negative comments up to your family and friends! Rather, the coach will say to you, what do you need to do to get to where you want to be? Do you need more training or experience? How long will it take? Are you willing to invest the time and possibly money to follow your dream?

Good coaches cost money so investing in coaching services is investing in your future. A good coach will know exactly when to hold your hand and when to kick your butt! They are also trained in the most current techniques that will save you hours of work and bring you faster, more reliable results. They are often the support you need to move forward, so don't discard the notion of hiring a coach too quickly.

Get recommendations from others, and above all, have an introductory session so that you can assess whether or not your personality and the coach's personality are compatible. This is critical, since you need to be comfortable talking with the coach and you need to feel you can trust that the coach will give you good advice. Remember, you can do anything with the right support!

2 Chapter Two
Job Search Survival 101

"It's only when we truly know and understand that we have a limited time on earth - and that we have no way of knowing when our time is up, we will then begin to live each day to the fullest, as if it was the only one we had."

- Dr Elisabeth Kubler Ross

Many of the strategies in this chapter mirror those in the previous chapter for a very good reason; they are worth repeating, and repeating, and repeating. Your attitude and your determination to conduct a proactive job search will mean the difference between landing a job quickly or not. You are in complete control of your attitude, beliefs and actions.

Whether you were just laid off from a job you loved, or one you hated, looking for a job when you were thrown into a state of joblessness, is challenging. It is often like riding on a Ferris wheel. There are days when you are up: you get up and you feel confident, knowing at your core who you are, what you do and which companies would need your expertise. On other days, you don't even want to get out of bed. You don't have a clue why anyone would even want to hire you!

Along with your highs and lows, your family is also experiencing highs and lows that may or may not correspond with yours. And so the Ferris wheel keeps going up and down, pitching your emotions up and down, as well. This is a very common scenario for the average job-seeker.

Is it hopeless? Of course not, but you need to be prepared for those down days. I encourage you to create a gameplan for the days when you are feeling blue. With some preplanning, you will be so prepared that you will gloss over those down days and immediately get out of the doldrums. Although everyone is entitled to a pity party after they have been laid off, it needs to be very short-lived. Long before you experience a down day, you need to create a plan that will clear your mood and get you ready to resume the job hunt right away.

On a day when you are feeling great, make a list of all the things you love to do, such as playing golf, taking walks on the beach, listening to music, taking a bubble bath. List all of the activities that bring you joy. Next, make a list of all the people who love just because you are who you are. You know, the people who make you laugh or who bring out the best in you. Finally, make a list of all of the places you love to go. Be creative and put as many things on your list as possible. Really spend the time thinking about the people, places and things that make you happy. If money is a concern, only list activities that are free such as a walk in the woods, reading a great book or taking a bubble bath.

Put your list in a safe place, but remember to get it out the moment you feel blue and make a commitment to yourself that no matter how sad you feel, you will choose something from your list and do it.

Another survival strategy is to find another job-seeker and brainstorm job search techniques. You can seek out a former colleague who has also been laid off, or you can look for a networking group to join. You can even strike up a conversation at a local coffee shop with someone sitting alone with a laptop.

Although, intuitively, searching for jobs is a competitive activity, many job-seekers seem to be very forthcoming with practical information on where to go to find new opportunities.

One of the very best survival skills is to stay in action. Often times inactivity creeps in when the job search seems to go nowhere, or your pipeline seems to be drying up. Be aware of what your daily activities are like. Get out of the house every day, exercise, give yourself permission to go to a movie occasionally or take a former colleague or supervisor out for coffee. The more active you stay, the better your chance of landing a new job sooner rather than later. Go to meetings like professional affiliation meetings. Part of everyday should include being with other people.

Another technique is to notice the questions you are asking yourself. Are you asking yourself "why" questions? Why did this happen to me? Why did they let me go? Why is it taking so long to find a new job? "Why" questions keep you stuck.

If you find yourself asking "why" questions, make a shift and ask yourself "how" questions instead. "How" questions move you toward solutions. Ask things like: "How can I connect with more organizations?" or "How can I leverage my skills to earn money now while I am looking for a permanent job?"

Simply by shifting your questions from "why" to "how" you will change the energy of your job search. You will go from frustration and possibly depression to action and hope. It is a powerful tool.

Another powerful technique for controlling your negative emotions is to assess how you feel and how you would rather be feeling. For example: "I am completely frustrated and I would rather be hopeful."

Next, close your eyes and think about a time when you were hopeful. Where were you? What brought you hope? Really tap into that feeling of hope. Visualize the scene. You now know that anytime you want to change a negative feeling you have regarding searching for a job, you have the ability to close your eyes and visualize that scene where you were hopeful. It is a powerful tool for shifting negative energy into positive energy that will move you into action. You can switch any negative emotion for a positive emotion by visualizing a time and place when you felt that positive feeling.

Finally, one of the most important techniques for having a successful job search is to have a great attitude. Know that there is an organization out there that really needs the skills you have developed. Be excited about the opportunity to work with new people who will be honored to work with you. Having a positive attitude will not only help you to sail through this period successfully, but is one of the key factors to landing a job when you get to the interview stage.

To recap for you, here are my top 10 favorite tools for surviving the ups and downs of a job search:

1. Create a game plan to use on days when you feel down.
2. Make detailed lists of your favorite activities, people and places.
3. Give yourself permission to have a very brief "pity party" if you need one, and then move on.
4. Partner with another job-seeker to brainstorm how to find new opportunities.
5. Stay in action.
6. Join networking groups and professional affiliation groups... be with people, especially people who are working in the industry you want to work in.
7. Get out of the house every day.
8. Shift from asking yourself "why" questions to asking "how" questions.
9. Practice visualizing the positive emotional states you want to be in.
10. Your attitude will determine your success. Stay positive!

3

Resumés

"Today a thousand doors of enterprise are open to you, inviting you to useful work." — Grenville Kleise

Your resume is your calling card. Many people feel that a resume should be a historical account of everything you have done since you got out of college and started your career. This isn't completely true. The real purpose of a resume is simply to get you an interview.

The resume you prepare when applying for a job should be a two-page dynamic document that highlights your accomplishments. When a hiring manager or Human Resources professional reads it, they should say: "I need to talk with this person!"

My rule of thumb is that if you have worked less than five years, you should have a one-page resume. If you have been in the working world for more than five years, yours should be a two-page document. If you are in certain industries such as education or medicine, and you have been published, you should have curriculum vitae (cv), which is a document that includes your resume and all of your publications. If you are an IT professional and have half a page of languages, software programs, etc. on your resume it can be two and a half pages.

I often tell my clients that I feel they should keep a historical document that lists EVERYTHING they have done. Include every class, certification, training program, etc. in their career.

This document is a great reference document for you, but must never be sent out. It can be twenty pages long, but it will never land you an interview!

Resumes come in two basic formats: reverse chronological and functional. I have rarely encountered anyone who understands a functional resume. Although they should be helpful to those who want to change careers, I never suggest that my clients use this format. They don't seem to deliver the desired results.

The top third of the first page of your resume is critical, so spend some time writing a dynamic professional summary that will paint an accurate picture of the kind of employee you are. If your summary is well written, the Hiring Manager should know whether or not he/she wants to interview you even before they read the rest of your resume. If you have a big spirit and are outgoing and action-oriented, be sure to include some dynamic action words in your summary. Really capture the essence of who you are in the summary.

Although, many do not feel it necessary to have multiple versions of your resume, I like the idea of having a targeted resume. By that I mean, use the summary and the "demonstrated strengths" section to target your resume for a specific job. You will then need to save that version as the company's name and your last name.

Since the majority of a resume is your history of work, education, technical skills, and professional affiliations, the only part of the resume that you need to change each time is the professional summary section. Use that initial section on your resume to leverage yourself to get noticed. Filter in some of the "buzz words" from the job posting. However, if something does not pertain to you or your abilities, never put it on your resume. Honesty matters.

When writing a resume, should I list my accomplishments on a separate page?

No, this is too confusing. List the accomplishments under the title you held when you had that accomplishment, and remember to bullet the accomplishments in the format that highlights what you did and how you added value to those with whom you interacted. Did you add value to a team, a client, the management or the organization as a whole? Highlight your accomplishments. Each bullet tells a brief story in two or three lines of text – no more. Keep it concise and direct: actions and value added or results.

You want six bullets for your most recent job and only three bullets for older jobs. Employers pay the most attention to your most recent job and look at former positions as stepping stones.

Often when writing the bullets on a resume, people repetitively use what I refer to as "security blanket" words. For example, those in Information Technology use words like "developed" or "implemented". Although what they do is develop and implement, reading those words over and over on a resume is very boring to the reader. One way to avoid that problem is to begin every bullet with the accomplishment or value added and then tell the actions or strategy used for getting there.

Your goal is to produce a dynamic, two page document that will get you an interview.

Should I have two versions of my resume, one to submit to recruiters and one to the Human Resource Department?

This is completely unnecessary. Technically, you should only need one version of your resume. You may want to change your summary to target a particular position for which you are qualified, but you shouldn't need to change the bullets. Remember, the bullets are your accomplishments, they shouldn't change.

You have the option of resubmitting a newer version to a recruiter as you make changes, but it truly feels like bait and switch if you try to send multiple versions of your resume to an employer. I highly discourage this practice. It is far better to wait a bit and clean up your resume before applying for a job rather than submit your resume too soon and want to send a newer version after your first submission. It really sends the wrong message to the Hiring Manager.

Where on the resume should I put community service?

Community service should be placed at the very end of your resume. Only include current community service projects. If you haven't volunteered for an organization in the past five years, do not include it on your resume.

It is also important that you do some research on the companies to which you are applying. If the company is very actively engaged in community service, including community service on your resume may be helpful in landing the job. On the other hand, if you do lots of community service and the organization does none, your efforts may be viewed as a distraction to your work, and eliminating the community service piece from your resume, may be the smarter choice. Do your research and let your resume work for you.

How far back should I identify employment on my resume?

In general, fifteen years should be enough, but many people have worked for an organization for more years than that, so use your judgment.

It is best, in a two-page document, to try not to have too many red flags. By this I mean, do not make statements such as: *Thirty years experience in...* Rather, say: *Extensive expertise in the areas of...*

Red flags that point to age should be avoided. Don't be eliminated from candidacy before the Hiring Manager gets the chance to interview you. Use your resume to leverage your abilities to do a job without making age an issue. If, after you are interviewed, a Hiring Manager does not choose to hire you, that's fine, the fit isn't there, but don't contribute to being eliminated by making age an issue.

Your primary goal should be to get an interview. If, after an interview you are not chosen, that is okay, but don't put up a wall before you even get in the door!

How do I justify a title change in a former organization where my title went to a lower level due to a re-organization within the company?

This is one of the hardest situations to handle on a resume. Usually at the time of the re-organization, your supervisor told you "nothing would change." Your responsibilities and your salary would remain the same, "just your title would change."

That's all well and good as long as you remain at that organization, but if you are part of a lay off later on, having what appears to be a demotion on your resume can hurt your chances of getting an interview. I will clarify this by saying that I don't think a lower level title will hurt you if you change organizations, i.e. moving from a smaller company to a larger one, or even changing departments within a company. The only time it becomes a red flag on your resume is when you stay in the same department and your title seems to go down in status.

One way to handle this is to put both your higher level and lower level title on the same line and just write one responsibilities statement that will include the duties for both titles. There should only be one set of bullets. This way, the drop in status will not seem so obvious to the reader.

What is the next step if I have been referred to a company by some of their employees, but have never heard from anyone in the Human Resources department or from a Hiring Manager?

I've included this question in the chapter on resumes although it could also be included in the chapter on networking because this is an example of how to handle the distribution of your resume. Whenever anyone asks for your resume, you need to ask them to whom they plan to give it and if they would share the contact information with you. It is important that you thank the person for being willing to share your resume with a Hiring Manager, but you need to tell them that you do not want to impose, nor do you want them to serve as your recruiter. Try to get the contact information of the person to whom they plan to give your resume so that you can follow up with that person. Many people mean well, and offer to pass your resume on, however, they often get busy and your resume may sit at the back of their desks for an extensive amount of time. By the time they realize they still have it and have done nothing with it, they may be too embarrassed to tell you or to even pass it on. Try to get control of where your resume is going and the follow through process.

Unfortunately, if you do not have any contact information and you haven't heard from anyone at the company, there is little you can do to gain visibility in the organization. The only hope for success is to use LinkedIn® to try to network your way into the company.

4

The Interview

"Promote your uniqueness, not your sameness."
- Angela Schutz

Interviews come in many formats. You may have a screening interview, a phone interview, a behavioral interview, a panel interview or a case interview. All forms of interviewing seem to be stressful to the job-seeker. I often remind my clients that the one thing to remember is that you should never go on an interview with the attitude that you are a lamb going to slaughter!

Remember that if you are invited in for an interview, it is an indication that the company feels you are competent to do the job. Hiring Managers do not waste time interviewing people who are not competent. They actually want you to land the job. You should be jumping for joy every time you land an interview. Walk into the interview with your head held high and the air of confidence you should have because you know they want you!

I often remind my job-seeking clients that a love affair is about to happen. Some company will want you, and you will fall in love with them! What could be better than knowing your new employer is excited about your skills and can't wait to have you start, especially after you have had to endure the stress and pain of a layoff?

I can't stress enough the importance of staying positive during the interview process. Companies take much longer, than the average job-seeker can bear, to decide which candidate to hire. If you focus on looking at the entire process as a way to find the right fit, you will realize that you need to take an active part in evaluating that fit. It is as important for you to decide that the company is right for you, as it is for the company to decide that you are the right candidate for the job.

There are a few things to remember when going on an interview:

1. Be on time or early, but do not arrive more than 15 minutes before your appointment. Having a candidate "hang around" the office is stressful for the hiring organization.

2. Turn your cell phone off. You don't want a call to catch you off guard.

3. Be sure you do not have gum in your mouth.

4. Bring a copy of your resume with you.

5. Bring a note pad, but do not focus on taking too many notes. You want to seem engaged with what the interviewer is saying.

6. Know what is on your resume and be able to speak to your accomplishments.

7. Know as much as possible about the hiring organization. What is their mission, vision, or product? Who are their customers? Do your research!

8. Have some open-ended, thought-provoking questions ready to ask the interviewer.

9. If at the end of the interview you are still interested in the position, then say so. Job-seekers who say they are still excited about the position get hired more often.

10. Write a thank you note within 24 hours. This is key to your success. Be sure you get the names and contact information from all of the people who interview you. You may write one note that thanks each person by name, but if there was a particular person that seemed to be in your corner during the interview, you may want to take the time to send that person a separate note.

11. If the Administrative Assistant was involved in setting up your interview, be sure to send her/him a thank you note, as well.

What are the top five things I should focus on to prepare for an interview?

There is an endless list of things you could prepare for prior to going on your interview, but the top five are:

1. Study the job posting and be able to demonstrate how or where you have gotten the education and/or the experience to do that part of the position.

2. Be prepared to name the top five achievements of your career.

3. Study the company's website so that you know what their mission and vision statements are and you can name such things as what they produce (or what type of service they offer) and who they serve (their customers).

4. Be prepared to clearly articulate why you are looking for a position and who you are professionally. Include your areas of expertise and unique strengths. This piece takes practice because for many of us, we were raised not to brag or boast, and when we get to an interview we are asked to tell a potential employer all about who we are. Practice this until you can find the words that you are comfortable using. Rather than starting every sentence with "I", you might want to soften things by saying something

like this: *Some areas in which I have had success are...* and then provide them.

5. Ask the person who set up the interview for some additional information such as how long your interview will be, will you be interviewed by one or more than one person, will you have a private interview with each person or will it be panel style, who will interview you and will business cards be provided for you?

Knowing who will interview you and other details such as how long and what style the interview will be in will help you to prepare well and be relaxed and confident. It will also give you the opportunity to look on LinkedIn® to gather information on the people who will interview you. We all feel more comfortable when we know someone, so take the time to "get to know" the interviewers in advance. It will pay off because you will seem more confident and hopefully will be able to point out some commonalities between you and the interviewers such as going to the same college or formerly being employed at the same organization.

Always remember that in an interview situation, the interviewer is only interested in what you can do for them. WIIFM is the acronym for "what's in it for me?" They are not interested in what the position will do to move your career forward. Don't talk about things such as the company is close to your home, you want to work closer to home because you have young children, or this job would look great on your resume.

Use every opportunity during the interview to promote your uniqueness, not your sameness, and answer each question in a way that helps the interviewer see you doing the job. You are given very little time to show how you have the skills to meet their needs. Be prepared with concrete answers that highlight all you bring to the table.

Is there any way I can have some control over the interview process?

The interview process is really in the hands of the hiring organization. They decide who to interview and how many interviews each candidate will be given.

You do, however, have some control over how the interview is going. You should try to keep all of your answers focused, so that the interviewer can, by your answers, picture you doing the job at their organization. You should also try to focus the interview if the interviewer talks so much that you never get the opportunity to answer a question. You can talk about how excited you are about the position and how your skills will have a positive effect on the work at hand.

One trick that helps is to mirror the pace and style of the interviewer. If they say things like: What are the top three skills you bring to the table? They are looking for a bulleted list. On the other hand, if they talk and give anecdotal stories, they want an answer from you that includes examples.

Your goal is to clearly link your skills with their posted needs. Even if you can do a higher level job, you need to only discuss the job at hand since it is the only thing the hiring manager has to offer.

The job posting is your best friend – know it well!

Another way to be successful on an interview is to increase your chances of having the Hiring Manager like your chemistry. You need to prepare some great, thought-provoking questions to ask. Interviewers seem to like us better when we draw them into the conversation.

How do I handle an interview that is scheduled on "dress down" Friday?

You only have one opportunity to make a good first impression. If the organization has indicated that your interview will be on "dress down" Friday, you should still dress in business casual clothes. You are always being evaluated on how well you attend to details. Never wear jeans to an interview. It doesn't matter what day of the week it is, you should be well dressed. It shows a great deal of respect when you dress well for the interview. I love the expression: *Dress for the job you want, not for the job you have.* You are always sending out messages about the type of employee you will be. Employers notice everything.

How much personal information should I reveal on an interview if asked?

If the interviewer asks personal questions that make you uncomfortable, such as whether or not you are married or have children, you can deflect the questions by saying: *"If you are asking me about the status of my family because there will be a good deal of traveling for this job, I can assure you that I will not have any problem keeping the commitments of the position".* You are not obliged to answer personal questions.

There are clearly questions pertaining to age, race and religion that are off limits, and even illegal, but although you shouldn't have to encounter them, you may, on occasion, find that an interviewer pushes the limits. Only answer questions that you are comfortable answering. If you feel threatened or insulted by a question, you can deflect it by saying something like: "Can you tell me how the date of my graduation will have an effect on my ability to do this job?"

After an interview, how often should I follow up to try to convince the hiring manager that I am the right candidate?

This is one of those, "It depends" type of answers. Listen to what the Hiring Manager is saying about the interview process. If they have said that they are interviewing candidates or that they won't make a decision for two months, then you can call back every two weeks. If there is a recruiter involved, you may certainly ask the recruiter how often you may contact them. Perhaps you can touch base once per week, or if things are nearing the deadline, every three days.

You certainly need to stay on their radar and show you are still interested in the position, but beware of being viewed as a "stalker"! Don't overdo it with regard to the frequency of your calls.

What do I have to do differently in an interview for an out of state position?

Be sure that it is a position you really want. You can bring up that relocation isn't a problem for you. If it is a problem, find a way to let the Hiring Manager know that you have thought about the distance and have figured out how you will be able to work with the organization despite the distance.

One thing you should always have clarity around is why you are applying for the position. If it is clearly the right job for you, but in the wrong location, you can negotiate the details surrounding how you can do the job, but the negotiations are best done after the organization has decided that they really want you and your skill set.

At an interview, how much should I disclose about other positions for which I am interviewing at alternate organizations? This is a case of less is more. You are under no obligation to talk about other potential jobs for which you are applying. However, if you are in a situation where job number one is moving slowly, and job number two seems like there will be an offer, don't panic. Go to the Hiring Manager for the position you want and ask them if they want to be told if you get a job offer. This will help you to know how serious the people are about hiring you and it may speed up their process, especially if they really want you. Don't do this if there really isn't another job offer in the works. You should never try to strong arm anyone into trying to get them to give you an offer.

How do I evaluate whether or not I am qualified for a position?

Start with the job posting. A job posting is traditionally set up with three identifiable areas: the responsibilities of the position, the wish list (MBA, bi-lingual, etc.) and the requirements for the position. Assessing your qualifications is a process of checking off all of the elements on the job posting that pertain to you.

Look over the entire posting and make note of all the requirements, wish list items and responsibilities with which you have had experience. Next, it's a simple exercise in arithmetic. Add up all of the check marks and if you can do 80% of what they are looking for, you can appropriately apply for the position. Hiring Managers are looking to hire employees who have the education, the experience or a combination of both.

Is it ethical to go on an interview if I am not interested in the position?

Yes, of course it is, if you go into the interview with an open mind. Interviews are exploratory conversations that help both you and the organization determine whether or not there is a good fit between you both. At times, when you are being interviewed for one position, it is determined that you would be a better fit for a different position within the organization. It may be a position that you had no idea existed. It would be terrible if you had decided not to go on the interview because you were not interested in the position and lost out on a great opportunity that wasn't obvious at the start of the process.

How should I handle the "overqualified for the position" statement from the Human Resources person or the Hiring Manager on an interview?

Very often the term "over qualified" is synonymous with too old. I don't know any organization that doesn't need someone who is "over qualified." Many times, as we move toward the end of the career spectrum, we are not given the same opportunities to straighten things out.

Look at this question of being over qualified as an opportunity to shine. This is your chance to highlight not only the wealth of experience you have, but the integrity, work ethic and sense of responsibility with which you will do the job. It is extremely important that you also show that you have a passion for the position. The passion piece is often the element that helps the Hiring Manager make the decision to choose you. All employers want employees who have both the qualifications and the motivation to do a job. If you have both, leverage that in your response to this question.

How far down the path do you go ethically before you reject an offer?

This is an interesting question because it is vital to the hiring process that you demonstrate your ability to negotiate. That being said, a reasonable request for more benefits during the hiring process shows your business acumen and often becomes the tie breaker between candidates, however, asking for too many things or benefits that have never been a part of the organization can take you down the wrong path and get you eliminated as a candidate for a position.

Once you start down the path of negotiating for more, it indicates that you are serious about the position. Once you have the initial offer and you have entered a counter offer, and if the organization comes back with an acceptance of your proposed offer, then the ethical thing to do is to accept the offer. Don't go down the path to negotiations if you are not serious about taking the job.

How can I delay giving an organization an answer to a job offer when I am waiting for offers from other organizations?

The hiring process takes a very long time, therefore when you are given an offer, you do not have to worry about asking for a bit of time to review the offer. Most employers expect that you will read the acceptance letter and after your review, you will make your decision.

You may even want to negotiate something in the offer letter before you accept it. It is not unreasonable to ask for anywhere from forty-eight hours to one week before providing your answer.

What is the appropriate process for following up with an HR person who did not show up for a prearranged interview?

Always take the high road. If an HR person stands you up, give them the benefit of the doubt because there must be a good reason, however, you still need to talk with them and be interviewed for a position, so send them an email or give them a call and say that you are sorry they were unable to make the appointment you had because you know they wanted to talk with you. Give them some dates and times when it would be best to reach you, and just wait for a response. As hard as it may be, you need to stay focused on why you need them and stay calm. You will really eliminate all opportunities to get interviewed if you make the HR person angry!

How much time should I allow between contacts to the Human Resource department?

If you have already had an interview, it is fine to call or email the HR contact once per week, but the time table should expand to once every two weeks if you have applied for a job, but have not yet been interviewed.

How do I handle a potential "no" and save face?

When actively pursuing new employment, it is important to remember several things. First, the interview process should be as much about finding out if the company is the right fit for you as it is finding out if you are the right fit for the position. Fit is the operative word! There should be no shame or "saving face" involved in the process.

At the conlusion of the interview if either you, or the hiring manager feel you are not the right candidate for the position, you should move on. The end result is that you are no worse off if the opportunity is not the right opportunity for you. If you did not have a job prior to the interview, and the interview did not result in a new position, you are exactly where you were before the interview. You are no worse off.

The other thing to remember is that there is no shame in any of this process. As a matter of fact, the more you can eliminate negative self-scripts, the faster you will land a new position. Concentrate on your strengths and finding a way to tell the next hiring manager what you bring to the table that will meet the needs they have. Your new mantra should be: *I will promote my uniqueness not my sameness.*

What is the appropriate amount of time to wait to follow up on a potential job offer after having the first interview?

Before the recession began in 2008, my answer would have been three weeks. My answer has changed as job scarcity is on the rise as is the competition for those jobs. There are times when the Human Resources contact will tell the applicant when to expect a call back, or when they should call the hiring organization. If, however, you do not have any idea, you should follow through in two weeks or less.

As you go on more and more interviews with the same company, the time between contacts needs to be shortened. You always want to stay on the radar screen of the Hiring Manager. Remember, you want to keep your interactions up, but you never, never want to be viewed, by the hiring organization, as a stalker. Your chances of losing the job opportunity increase exponentially as you abuse conventional communication guidelines.

How do you answer the question from the hiring manager: What have you been doing while you have been out of work?

With so many fabulous employees in the job pool, you need to leverage yourself to make a good impression on your interview. One way to do that is to do something concrete that will increase your skills while you are out of work. Take a course or study the technology for the industry you work in, so that your skills will stay sharp, even if you have been out of work for a few months. This will have multiple benefits: it will impress your next employer when you are on an interview and it will give you something positive to do that will help to keep your spirits up while you look for a new job.

If you qualify for unemployment insurance, you may also qualify for government education assistance. Check with your state's Department of Labor website to verify your qualifications to get financial assistance to get the education you need to be retrained for a new career or industry.

How can I effectively evaluate the risk of a new and frightening opportunity?

The simple answer to this question is "go with your gut." If an opportunity seems too good to be true, or it is in the wrong location, it will create an enormous commute or any other scenario, it is often best to get out a piece of paper and create two columns: Positives and Negatives of taking this job. List absolutely everything you can think of and either put the item in the positive or negative column. It will soon be revealed to you as to whether or not this is a good opportunity for you to accept.

Even if your list of positives is greater than your list of negatives, you may experience some feelings of doubt. Scan the feelings in your body when you think about the job. If your body is telling you that something just isn't right, listen to it. Our bodies send us wonderful signals that help us make the right decisions. Listen to your body and do not take a job when your body tells you it is the wrong opportunity for you. Going with your gut is usually the right approach.

What is the best way to search out how to set appropriate fees for consulting positions?

Many "seasoned" clients who have been in the workforce for a long time feel that consulting is the right next step before retirement. They have so much knowledge and experience with an industry that they want to try their hands at consulting. They initially have a difficult time figuring out how much they should charge per hour for a consulting position.

One of the easiest ways to get an initial rate is by figuring out what you were making in salary last year and divide the total by 2080 hours. The figure you come up with is an average hourly wage. You can then add up to 30% to take in account additional benefits that the hiring organization will not pay a consultant.

Alternately, you can use salary calculators and plug in the title and location to get an estimated salary figure. You should plug in that title for several different cities to calculate an average. You can then divide that figure by 2080 to arrive at an hourly figure.

How do I handle the "stress" question?

Often when you are on an interview, you are asked how you handle stress. Nearly everyone says things like: *I am fine with stress, as a matter of fact, I work really well when I have close deadlines and am in a fast-paced environment.*

Sometimes the interviewer will continue to ask you questions and after you have, in your estimation, answered the question well, they will then stop talking. This is a great technique for putting the applicant into a stressful situation!

Don't cave in and don't start trying to fill the dead air space with nervous chatter. Just embrace the silence for a short while and then, very calmly, ask if there is anything you can do to clarify your last answer. You will come off as very confident rather than as an individual who comes unraveled easily.

What's the best way to prepare for an interview?

There are many ways to prepare for an interview:

1. Study the organization's website.

2. Know the job posting inside out and backwards!

3. Ask others to share what they know about the organization.

4. Look up the people who will interview you on LinkedIn®.

5. Look for any areas on the job posting where you have not had much experience or that you did so long ago that it does not show up on your resume. Before you go for the interview, prepare an answer that addresses how you will handle that part of the job. A good interviewer will ask you about every part of the position, so don't overlook any part of the posting when preparing. Create a story that shows how you handle challenges in the workplace or in your life. Don't play ostrich and think they won't ask. Be prepared.

What many people do not realize is that the interview process is much like playing poker. Everyone wants to hold their cards close to their chest. For you, the job-seeker, this is important information that can certainly help you land at the very least, a second interview.

Let's look at a typical interview scenario: you, the job-seeker, are called in to be questioned by the Hiring Manager. The thing you don't know is whether you are the first candidate or the last. The Hiring Manager may think you are a fantastic candidate, but if there are four more candidates that still need to be interviewed; the Hiring Manager needs to "keep his cards close to the chest" and not reveal anything to you because of the upcoming interviews he needs to conduct.

You, on the other hand, can and should reveal, at the end of the interview, that you are still interested in the position. It seems simplistic, but this is your opportunity to set yourself apart from the rest of the candidates. Often, at the end of the interview, you are asked if you have any questions. The answer is ALWAYS "yes". This is your opportunity to show your passion for the position by saying something like: "Now that we have fully discussed this position, I am even more excited about this opportunity because I would be able to use my skills in (name the skills you have for the position) to have a positive impact on (state the needs of the position)."

Remember that if you are fortunate enough to get an interview put your cards on the table and if you are still interested in the position at the end of the interview, say so! Let them offer the job to you rather than to the candidate who is a "poker face."

5

Informational Interviews

*"The true way to render ourselves happy is to
love our work and find in it our pleasure."*

— Francoise de Motteville

Informational interviews are a wonderful way to get Hiring Managers to know you are out there looking for a new position. I often remind my clients that, as a job-seeker, your goal is to get yourself in front of as many people in the power to hire you as possible. Be aware that the person who needs you probably doesn't know you are out there and available.

One of the best ways to do that is to request an informational interview. This powerful networking tool has been known to accelerate one's ability to land a job, but there are some ground rules to which you must adhere.

What are the guidelines for an informational interview?

Here are six to consider:

1. Ask for a moderate amount of time in which to meet and, no more than thirty minutes. I once read an article that suggested a 12-minute meeting because it showed the Hiring Manager that you were respectful of his/her busy schedule and, that no one would forget a person who asked for twelve rather than fifteen or thirty minutes!

2. Have a copy of your resume with you, but be sure your intent is clearly focused on sharing industry knowledge – not ambushing the person by asking for a job!

3. Prepare three or four questions. Remember, twelve minutes is not a lot of time.

4. Never leave the informational interview without trying to obtain another networking contact.

5. You must serve as the time keeper. This is crucial! As it nears the end of the pre-arranged time, you need to state that you see the time is nearly up and thank the person for taking time out of their busy day to talk with you. Also, ask if it is permissible for you to follow up with them by email if you have any additional questions. Your reputation will skyrocket with the Hiring Manager because you are remaining true to your word. You are also giving them the opportunity to wiggle out of a meeting with you that isn't going well, or if they no longer have time to continue. The added benefit is that many times, if the Hiring Manager is enjoying the conversation and does not have a pressing commitment, he/she may suggest you continue your discussion.

6. This is the most crucial part of an informational interview: Never ask for a job. It is vital to your success that you don't ambush the Hiring Manager. Your purpose is to get noticed, have an industry discussion and try to get another networking contact, nothing more!

The bottom line is that, in essence, you have just had your first interview with the Hiring Manager and you are now the known candidate when a position becomes available!

How do I go about landing an informational interview?

Networking can really come into play here. Ask people you know who work in organizations that interest you if they can introduce you to the Hiring Manager in the department for which you have appropriate skills. You can also attempt to call an organization and try to get to the highest level employee that you can reach. You can tell them that you are at the crossroads of your career and are gathering industry information. Ask if they would meet with you for a brief meeting, such as the "twelve minute" meeting.

6

Chapter Six

Phone Interviews

"A master in the art of living draws no sharp distinction between his work and his play; his labor and his leisure; his mind and his body; his education and his recreation. He hardly knows which is which. He simply pursues his vision of excellence through whatever he is doing, and leaves others to determine whether he is working or playing. To himself, he always appears to be doing both."

— Francoise Rene Auguste Chateaubriand

I recently had the pleasure of hearing Paul Bailo from Phone Interview Pro (www.phoneinterviewpro.com) speak to an audience of job-seekers who are all recently unemployed and in the process of seeking new employment. I thought the materials were very well-received and helped the clients to solidify the points we have been trying to teach them on the importance of being clear and concise in an interview.

Paul's delivery is excellent! He treats each and every audience member as if they are special and encourages their participation in the workshop. As a Career Counselor, I always worry about how information is received by clients. Much to my surprise, two weeks after the Phone Interview Pro workshop, I was talking with a group of clients and they brought up the point that they had learned how important it is to really prepare for the phone interview. They were quoting, verbatim, some of the techniques they had learned from the workshop.

I spoke with Paul and asked him to give me some tips that would help my clients and those reading this book.

Here is his response:

"The keys to conducting a world class phone interview are:

1. Be Yourself At Your Best
2. Be Brief - Be Bold - Be Done
3. Tell The Person How You Feel... *I am Passionate About This Job*, or *I Love What Your Organization Is Doing To Help People*, etc.

Good Luck and Don't Give Up!"

- Paul Bailo - CEO Phone Interview Pro

In this volatile job market, we all need to learn unique tips that will help us stand out from other applicants, so that we can land the job. Look for opportunities to learn new techniques that will enhance your job search techniques. Taking a workshop strictly devoted to teaching you how to be successful on a phone interview is a wonderful way to enhance your skills.

Phone interviews have become a huge part of the job search process. Many organizations use the phone as a way to provide a first screening opportunity. It usually saves them money, unless they hire a screening organization to perform the service, and it is an efficient way to assess the applicant's ability to perform the job.

There are both positives and negatives for the applicant associated with the phone interview process. Some of the positives include: your ability to have all of your pertinent documents at your fingertips when you interview, easy access to your computer and the internet if the interviewer asks you a question regarding the organization that you do not readily know. Some of the negatives are that although you may be less nervous because you are not directly in front of the interviewer, they cannot see you either, and are missing out on valuable visual and non-verbal signals that may increase your ability to connect with them. Additionally, your inability to see them may make you feel like you are talking into thin air, therefore, you may sound less passionate for the job than you actually are.

One must treat the phone interview with as much importance as a face-to-face interview. I have heard many clients tell me: *"I only have a phone interview."* This is the wrong attitude because the phone interview is the FIRST STEP in the successful landing of a new job!

Whether you have a phone interview with a recruiter; a screening organization that was hired by your potential new employer; or by the new Human Resources professional or Hiring Manager of the company treat it with the same weight and respect as you would an in-person interview. The preparation should be exactly the same and you should approach it with the same energy and drive you have for in-person interviews.

How should I prepare for a phone interview?

In many ways, the preparation for a phone interview is the same as that for a face-to-face interview. Here's 8 preparation strategies:

1. Research the company and those who will interview you.

2. Have all of your career success stories ready. You may want to write them out on 3x5 cards so they can be at your fingertips.

3. Be prepared to answer the question: Why should I hire you?

4. Know your professional introduction so that you can say it comfortably and confidently.

5. Get up early and practice talking so that your voice is strong and you don't sound sleepy. You might even want to have a hard candy or cough drop (Paul Bailo) before the interview, as well.

6. Be able to name the top five accomplishments of your career.

7. Have your resume, cover letter, job posting, etc. in front of you when you are on the phone, so that you can comfortably answer any question you are asked.

8. Have a photo of the person who will interview you in front of you. You may want to download it from LinkedIn®. That way you will be better able to connect with them.

The beauty of a phone interview is that you can have everything in front of you rather than being challenged to remember everything like you are in a face-to-face interview.

The challenge is to convey passion and excitement for the job without any visual signs. One thing you can do is use your voice to convey interest and passion. Pick up the pace with which you speak during parts of the interview to show excitement. You can also use the technique of mirroring the pace and style of the interviewer. It is a good way to have that person bond with you more.

One of the most important things to remember is that a phone interview should have as much importance in your mind as a face-to-face interview. Do not shortchange it. I hear so many people say: "I only have a phone interview". Remember that the phone interview is often the only path toward getting a face-to-face interview and potentially the job. Take it seriously and be thrilled that you were invited to talk with the organization!

7

Interview Questions
How To Answer Them and Ask Them

"I have learned that if one advances in the direction of his dreams, and endeavors to live the life he has imagined, he will meet with a success unexpected in common hours."

— Henry David Thoreau

Let's talk about the interview and your path to success. We've talked about the variety of types of interviews, but what we need to do now is roll up our sleeves and talk about the questions that sometime derail us in the interview process.

So many times, as soon as you walk out the door from an interview, you think: *"I should have said this* _____*!"* If you have ever experienced frustration over how you answered questions in an interview, you are not alone, and more importantly, there is something very simple you can do that will increase your ability to think faster and respond more accurately as interview questions are being fired at you.

Think about it, the hardest part of the interview process is that you are being called upon to think on your feet. You could easily "ace" any interview if the Hiring Manager would simply give you the questions in advance.

You would come up with a scenario to demonstrate your abilities related to the question and answer with ease. You also know that everything gets better with practice. Why not combine a form of interview practice with mastering the ability to "think on your feet"? My suggestion is simple but has had a powerful effect on my clients' success rate in landing a job.

When you know that you have an upcoming interview, enlist the help of trusted family and friends. Tell them you have an interview coming up in a few days and you need them to ask you interview questions. Here's the trick, tell them that you want them to surprise you with the questions.

Give them a reference time such as 9:00 am – 5:00 pm and ask them to simply ask you an interview question, listen to your answer, and , if you trust their judgment, give you some feedback in this format: *"What worked well for me is and what would have worked better is _____."* It is really important you practice how to answer questions with ease, and this process will help to perfect your answers and avoid the frustration associated with forgetting to highlight accomplishments that appropriately answer the question and illuminate your ability to do the job at hand. Simple, right? It is truly one of the most effective ways to develop your self-confidence before you go on the interview.

What kind of questions can I expect to be asked on an interview?

The first question is usually: "Tell me about yourself." This seems like an innocent enough question, but many job-seekers bore the interviewer by going into too many details or by going back too far in their careers. No one wants to hear about what you did twenty years ago! Hopefully you have grown significantly since then.

That question should more appropriately be stated: "Tell me how your experiences and skills will have a positive impact on this position? My rule of thumb is to answer absolutely every question in a way that allows the Hiring Manager to "see" you actually doing the posted job. He/She doesn't really want to know that you were born in Toledo and love Labrador Retrievers! Unfortunately, too many job-seekers answer that question in a similar way. They fail to show their value as related to the job! Don't miss this golden opportunity to connect your skills to the job at hand.

The second question that is often asked is: *"Tell me why you are looking for work?"* If you were laid off from your last position, you need to prepare a positive statement about how, due to the economic downturn your company eliminated your position along with those of many of your colleagues. In some cases, your department was moved out of state and you were unable to relocate at this time, etc. Be honest, but don't create a scenario that looks like you were at fault for losing your job. It is really important that you also express how excited you are to take your vast knowledge and experience as a _____ (your title) to a new organization.

The two things you want to avoid are showing anger for your last organization and showing you feel to blame for your lay off. I truly believe that all Human Resources professionals and Hiring Managers develop a unique form of radar to detect the negative feelings job-seekers have. They hear the negative between the words you speak and they see it in your body language, so you need to leave any negativity you might harbor for being laid off, at the door!

Take some time to really see the gift you have been given by no longer being at your former organization. There is often a hidden gift in every difficult situation. When you take some time to examine the situation, you may find that your lay off was a gift.

Clients have expressed things such as: *"I have an ill family member and my not working at the moment has allowed me to spend quality time with my loved one when they need my support most."*

"I was really unhappy (unfulfilled) there and they did me a favor. I am now free to find a new position that is more in alignment with who I really am."

In general, if you think about the qualities every organization wants in an employee, you can probably come up with a long list of questions they may ask you.

Questions may try to uncover such elements such as:

- Your qualifications to do the job

- Your technical skills as related to the position

- Your level of education

- Your motivation

- Your leadership qualities

- Your integrity, values, work ethic, etc.

- Your career aspirations

- Your collegiality

Another way to "unlock the mystery" of the interview process is to take the job posting and make a list of the responsibilities of the position, the additional preferences the organization wishes you had, such as an MBA degree or your ability to speak a second language, and the requirements for the position such as five years of industry experience.

Take the list you made and think of relevant questions for each item and how you would respond. You have the ability to demystify the interview process and, you should, so that you can successfully land that job!

The keys to interview success are to keep your answers relevant, but brief. Let the interviewer follow up with another question if they need a more detailed answer from you. Practice highlighting how your abilities, skills and knowledge (think of the acronym ASK) apply to the posted needs of the job.

Enlist the help of family and friends so that you can practice coming up with relevant answers to questions on the spot. More importantly, show your passion for the job and how your skills will make an immediate and positive impact on the position.

Another key to success is your ability to engage the interviewer in conversation. One of the best ways to do that is to have some great open-ended questions prepared that you can ask them.

Here are a few examples:

- If offered this position, how could I best support you (the Hiring Manager) to accomplish your goals for this department?

- What would be the most significant impact I could make in the first six months?

- Who is your ideal candidate for this position?

- What do you need to know about me that you have not yet heard to convince you that I am the right person for this position?

- What is the management style of this organization?

8

Chapter Eight

Salary

"You know you are on the road to success
if you would do your job, and not be paid for it."

— Oprah Winfrey

Salary is one of those topics that creates angst for the job-seeker and Hiring Manager alike, however, introducing it into the conversation is completely in the court of the Hiring Manager. As a job-seeker, you should never bring up the topic of salary while you are being interviewed. It is viewed as presumptuous for the job-seeker to initiate the salary conversation because as a job-seeker you do not know whether or not the employer is interested in hiring you.

Once the Hiring Manager has opened the conversation of salary, you, as the job-seeker should evaluate how you should answer the question of how much you are looking to make. Your answer should depend on where in the interview the topic comes up. I know that seems strange, but the timing of the question reveals how the Hiring Manager views you as a potential employee. If the "what are you looking to make?" question comes up at the very beginning of the interview, they are simply trying to eliminate candidates, as may be the case in the middle of the interview. If, however, the question is posed at the end of the interview, there is a strong possibility that the hiring organization is truly interested in you and is ready to negotiate to see if you can come to a mutual agreement and successful hire.

There are some tactics you can use to help deflect the question so that you are given the opportunity to impress the organization with your skills and insure they are interested in you before you engage in the salary discussion with them. You need to practice this so that your answers become comfortable for you to articulate. You don't want to run the risk of selling yourself short because you got nervous talking about money or because you had a flash of unworthiness because you are out of work.

Before you go on any interview, it is important for you to assess all of the accomplishments in your career so that you can speak to your strengths. It is as important to prepare for the salary question by researching current salaries for a similar title in your location and by going into the interview know three things:

1. What is your fall-off-the-chair dream salary?

2. What is a realistic salary for this title in this location?

3. What is the salary you need to walk away from because it won't support your family?

If you are prepared to answer all of these questions, then you will be ready to take on the salary negotiations. Remember that the timing of the salary question is as important as the preparation for the salary negotiations.

What is the best answer to the request for my salary history?

You can do several things that will help you avoid giving an exact number. One of the things I like best is to give a salary range. You can say: *My compensation package was between X dollars and X dollars ($00.00-$00.00).* You may include bonuses and other benefits, but should just give the figures without an explanation. When you simply say: *Last year my salary was X dollars*, you often hurt yourself especially if the benefits at the new organization are less than those of your former organization.

Ideally, you don't want to be the one to state the numbers. It is far better for the hiring organization to tell you what they are willing to pay. As soon as you state a figure, most of your negotiating power is gone!

At what point should I accept a low salary offer?

At no time should you accept an offer that you and your family cannot live on. When you begin searching for a new job, you need to spend some time reviewing your finances. You should do some research on job titles for which you are qualified and determine what are the typical salaries paid for that title in your location. The same title in different cities brings in very different salaries. There are many salary calculator systems on the internet that you can use for free. Do the research. Check the title in several cities to get a salary range.

The final, and most important, research you need to do is to review your finances and figure out your bottom line salary. You need to have a number in your mind as to what salary you cannot work for because it will not support your family and your lifestyle.

How should I respond when asked about salary and I ask for the range they had in mind for the position, only to be told, not to worry about the range, just tell them what I am looking for?

The salary question seems to haunt everyone. You have been told that once you say a number, your ability to negotiate a higher salary has ended. There are also some ways to deflect the question, especially if it is asked at the very beginning of the interview. When the hiring manager asks you what you are looking to make, and the question is at the very beginning of the interview, chances are that they are simply trying to eliminate candidates.

At the beginning, they do not know what your skills are and how you will add to their organization. At that point, you should attempt to deflect the question by saying: *Although salary is important to me, the fit is much more important, so if you don't mind, I'd rather discuss salary after we both agree that I am the best person for the job.*

When asked at the middle of an interview, what kind of salary am I looking to make, how shall I answer? Clearly, if you have been able to dodge the salary question at the beginning of the interview and they are asking that dreaded question yet again, you can say something like: I am sure you have a salary range in mind for this position; may I know what that range is?

Honestly, salary is a very sticky subject. There are times when you can ask a counter question and the organization will tell you the range for the position, without hesitation. At other times, they do not want anything other than to have you give them a flat out answer. You need to be able to take the temperature of the discussion and not push for their answer so hard that you lose the opportunity.

You should also go into the interview knowing what your previous compensation was for the past several years and what went in to making up that salary package.

Remember all salaries are not equal.

One of the main reasons for avoiding a direct answer regarding salary is that benefits hold tremendous weight in the final compensation package. If, for example, you made a six-figure income, had four weeks' vacation, a generous 401K matching package, and premium medical insurance at your former company, you should be reluctant to state a salary figure to your potentially new employer before you have the facts regarding the additional benefits you would be offered. That type of comparison is like comparing apples to oranges, you just can't do it.

9

Recruiters

"What is it that you like doing? If you don't like it, get out of it, because you'll be lousy at it. You don't have to stay with a job for the rest of your life, because if you don't like it you'll never be successful in it." — Lee Iacocca

What is it that you like doing? If you don't like it, get out of it, because you'll be lousy at it. You don't have to stay with a job for the rest of your life, because if you don't like it you'll never be successful in it.

Recruiters, I'd love to say you can't live with them, and you can't live without them, but of course you can, and more importantly, in many cases you should! I am a firm believer in an active job pursuit. By that I mean, you, the job-seeker, try your best, given all of the tools and techniques you know, to find a new position on your own through using a combination of job board research, industry research and networking. You should be actively engaged in the search for new employment. Very often, however, when people engage in working with recruiters they go into passive mode. They feel that because they have given all of their documents to a recruiter, they are still "looking for a job". In reality, they simply shut down. They let the recruiter do the work, and they complain if the recruiter doesn't contact them enough or doesn't get them in front of enough Hiring Managers.

It is important to remember that in times of a downturned economy where jobs are scarce, the recruiter is in the same situation as you. Simply put, there are fewer jobs and more applicants which lessens the opportunities for all applicants. If you are scanning the job boards and not finding many positions that interest you, chances are the recruiters are having similar difficulties trying to put you before hiring organizations.

Another thing to remember is that recruiters are people too. They go home at night and have families to feed just as you do and they work on commission. Tough economic times are hard on them too. Unfortunately, some recruiters do not take the high road and resort to unfavorable tactics simply to get you placed so that they can make their commission. Although there are many fabulous recruiters who work with high integrity and authentically love helping people land new positions, there are some who use questionable tactics to get you hired.

You need to do some research on the recruiter and the placement agency before you sign up with them. Ask lots of questions get referrals and by all means trust your inner guidance system to tell you whether or not you and the recruiter are a right fit. If, for any reason, you feel uncomfortable working with the recruiter, get out of the relationship. Evaluate whether or not you can conduct the job search on your own before you sign on with a recruiter.

Certainly there are some positions, especially at the higher executive level that will never be posted on a job board. In this case, you must engage the services of the recruiter who is handling the position. Be open with the recruiter and let them know who you are and why you are qualified for the position, and then take it a bit further by asking the recruiter to tell you what they plan to say about you. Having this type of discussion before the recruiter tries to present you to a Hiring Manager will help the recruiter to present you authentically and honestly. In the long run, it will be well worth the extra investment of time to ensure your success.

What should I do with a recruiter with whom I cannot connect?

Release them! If you cannot create a connection and if you feel the recruiter doesn't get you, it is of no avail to continue with them. Your goal is to get into the driver's seat with recruiters. You can do things like ask them sell you to you. It is vital that they understand you and your particular skill set so that they can present you to Hiring Managers. If they do not understand you or your capabilities, it is unlikely you will be chosen as the best candidate.

You should also ask the recruiter for the name and contact of another client that they have successfully placed so that you can assess whether or not you want to work with that recruiter, based, in part, on the experience of other candidates.

Lastly, look up the search firm with the Better Business Bureau to see if there are any complaints against the firm. Remember, you should not be too quick to hand over your resume and salary requirements to just anyone. Although you do not feel you are paying for the service, recruiters make good commission when they place a candidate, so you need to be a good consumer and treat this the same way you would treat any purchase of a service.

Do your homework! Look them up, research the quality and success of the service they provide, ask others for recommendations and get in the driver's seat. You owe that to yourself.

How can I convince a recruiter to present me if I am over qualified?

To expect a recruiter to present you for a position for which you are over qualified is a mistake. It is important not to go backwards in your job search. It is also extremely unlikely that you will be called in for an interview for a position that is far below the level you have most recently attained. The hiring organization would consider you a flight risk if they hired you. It would be assumed that you would leave the position as soon as a position came up that was both at your level and at your higher salary range.

The other factor that usually comes into play is your emotional state. You can't go back emotionally. Once you got into a lower level position, you would start to lament not being on a higher level. It is very hard to take a back seat role when you have previously led others to move an organization forward. Rather than spending an exorbitant amount of time pursuing lower level positions and badgering a recruiter to present you as a candidate, take a realistic approach by searching for positions for which you are appropriately qualified.

If a recruiter does not call me at a scheduled appointment time, should I call him?

Certainly, there may be a very good explanation why they didn't reach you. Don't create negative scripts in your mind to explain something you cannot know about. Quite often, we are so wounded when we are laid off that we create negative, damaging scripts so that we can feel even worse. Be good to yourself and know that the world is not out to get you. As a matter of fact, I love the concept from Jack Canfield's book, *The Success Principles*. In Principle 6: Become An Inverse Paranoid, he talks about the power we would gain simply by getting up each day and thinking that the entire world was plotting to help us!

Imagine how confident and supported you would feel if you felt everyone was trying to help you find your next job! As a matter of fact, when you start to adopt positive attitudes, the negative things seem to vanish into the background, and you automatically begin to notice all of the help and kindness others extend to you. Many of my clients have told me stories about people they hardly knew who came forth with great networking leads to help them during their job search.

How can I be sure a recruiter is effectively communicating my skills and needs to the Hiring Manager?

One of the most brilliant ideas I've heard in a long time came from one of my clients who takes his resume and a job posting for which he is qualified to a recruiter. He tells the recruiter that he will call him in a few days and ask him to sell my client to himself. It is a great way to find out whether or not the recruiter truly understands what you do. It will also demonstrate how the recruiter will present you to the Hiring Manager.

Should I push a recruiter to find out why I wasn't chosen for a position?

Although it would be a wonderful learning tool for you to understand why you didn't land a particular job, most of the time, the recruiter is reluctant to give you that information, even if he/she knows. Unfortunately, many job-seekers create so many negative scripts that they feel to blame for not landing a position, when there may have been nothing they could have done differently, they simply did not have the right combination of education and experience for the position. Don't stress over not knowing the why and practice how to link your best skills with the needs of a posted position.

One of my favorite quotes is:

> *"Other people's opinion of you is none of your business."*
>
> - Jack Canfield, The Success Principles

Don't stress out, just move on. There will be someone out there who really wants and needs you, just keep looking.

10

Your GPS For Navigating A Career Fair

"Do you want to know who you are?
Don't ask. Act! Action will delineate and define you."

— Thomas Jefferson

Here are some tools for successfully navigating a career fair. If you follow these simple ideas you will increase your visibility with the companies that interest you. It certainly can be daunting to have to walk into a room full of people, clutching your resume and trying to figure out what to say and do that will increase your chances of getting your next job. Career fairs are unique in that they are the only places where you can have access to many people at the same time, all with the power to hire you! They offer you the opportunity to impress the company's representative, especially if your resume does not stand out AND they help you to assess the company's culture based on the type of representative they send. It is simply a great idea for any job-hunter to go to career fairs, and yes, I know that if you are a seasoned employee who has had high-level positions in the past, you might think that career fairs won't have the level of jobs you are looking for, and you are right.

I would encourage you not to miss the most important aspect of the career fair: the ability to connect directly with company representatives who are often the decision makers for hiring new employees. If you are an executive, engage in conversation (an informal interview) and mention that you don't see any jobs at your level, but would they bring your resume back to the company and review it based on the higher level positions that may be coming up. Remember, a career fair has the potential of putting you in front of Hiring Managers from several companies all at once. There are some things to do in advance of attending the career fair that will increase your chances of getting noticed.

My favorite to-dos:

- Prepare your resume, proofread it twice and bring 25 copies with you (more if it is a very large career fair). Be sure your most current contact information is on you r resume.

- If you have access to the list of companies that will be in attendance, spend some time doing research on those companies in advance so that you can target the ones that most appeal to you.

- Have a plan for how you will use your time while at the career fair. Don't waste time talking to representatives who are from companies that you have no interest in. Start with the organizations that are at the top of your wish list.

- When looking for a job, you should always have a targeted approach: know the type of position you are looking for, the type of environment you prefer and what businesses are in the industry for which you are most qualified.

- Prepare your 30-second introduction that focuses on the unique benefits you can offer the employer - your unique professional introduction. Be brief. Be clear. Be confident.

- Don't wear perfume or cologne. Scents can be a real turn off, especially an entire room full of scents.

- Be prepared to talk about your skills, abilities and experiences in your industry. If you are a college student, you can expect questions about your field of study and your GPA.

- Since most of the hiring process involves screening of potential employees prior to the interview, take advantage of the face-to-face opportunity to meet employers. You will also have the opportunity to find out more about the company that isn't included in their website. Nothing replaces in-person contact for making a good impression!

- The companies are looking for good candidates. Show them that you are one by being curious. Prepare questions to ask that show you are knowledgeable about the company and the industry. Be prepared to answer basic interview questions such as: why should we hire you?

Questions to ask at a Career Fair

Here are a few questions you could potentially ask at a career fair, but if you really want to impress the company representative, be sure to ask them some questions you have developed from the information you have read on their website or from research you have done on the industry. NEVER ask questions like: So what does your company do? Do your research in advance and let your knowledge show through!

I am always reminded of the famous quote:

How do you get to Carnegie Hall? Practice. Practice. Practice.

The same is true here. Pick a few questions that you feel you could comfortably ask and practice. Confidence is key when searching for a new job and the best way to become confident is to plan, prepare and practice.

- What kinds of skills and experience do you look for in the employees you hire?

- Are graduate degrees important to advancing within your organization? Which ones?

- What are the characteristics of your most successful employees?

- Which courses or experiences do you suggest to be a successful candidate?

- Does your company hire on a continual basis or only at certain times of the year?

- How long does the hiring process take?

- What are the next steps?

- What percent of applicants are eventually hired?

- Are there career tracks within your organization?

- What kinds of positions (or internships) exist within your organization?

- Does the company promote from within?

- Can you tell me about your organization's culture?

- For how many years does the typical employee stay with the company?

- Are there opportunities for ongoing training through your organization?

- Do you expect your employees to relocate? How much travel is involved?

- What keeps you there?

Remember, if you go in to the career fair prepared with the knowledge of the companies that interest you and a plan for meeting the representatives you will have a successful plan for navigating the room. As in many of the chapters in this guide, I will remind you that your mindset is of the utmost importance. Go to the career fair with the attitude that the company that you will work for next is represented in that room and they need to meet you!

Another great networking technique that I've learned for working a room that is filled with people you don't know, and may be a bit intimidating, is to pretend that everyone there is at a party… your party. You are the host, and as the host, it is your responsibility to introduce everyone to each other. This networking technique really works. You go up to someone, introduce yourself, ask who they are and what they do. Next, turn to someone else in the room and introduce the person you just met to the second person. By the end of the night, everyone knows your name, and likes you because you made them feel so comfortable. Remember to enjoy the experience, knowing that it has the potential of getting you on the path to your next job.

11

Networking

*"Nobody cares how much you know
until they know how much you care."*

— Theodore Roosevelt

Networking, when done right, can be the key to landing your next job. Yet, so many people view it as a torturous ritual. All too many people pass up the opportunity to network with people they know because they feel embarrassed that they are looking for a job.

This is what I have come to learn and consequently love about networking. Networking is a process where someone who knows you and respects your work gives another person a great recommendation about you. If the person you know is well respected in their organization, the hiring manager is more likely to call you in for a discussion or interview. In fact, the more well-respected your contact is, the more the hiring manager expects to like you. It's the halo effect.

The piece of networking that most people don't consider is how wonderful your contact will feel if they are instrumental in getting you a new job. Plus, they may feel honored and validated because you respected them enough to ask them to help you.

What are the key points to get started with effective networking?

One of the most simplistic and effective ways to network is to say to someone: *"I am looking for a new opportunity in (name an industry, job function or even company name) with whom should I be talking?" "Can you facilitate my meeting them?"*

One thing I like to stress is the importance of having business cards made as soon as you are out of work. My apologies to the 3M Company, but I think there is nothing tackier than having someone ask you for your contact information and you reach for a post-it note or a scrap of an envelope!

Be the professional that you are and create simple business cards. You only need your name; some titles or functions you have held; an email address and phone number. Don't include complicated designs – keep it simple.

You can find several on-line sites that will give you 250 business cards for free. You only have to pay for the postage.

How do I pick the right networking group?

First, evaluate what you are looking for in a networking group. Remember that although many networking groups bring you a bit of social networking along with job search opportunities, if you are looking for a social life; join another type of group, not a networking group.

Second, if you have worked with a career counselor and have learned a great deal about the job search process, you will be coming to that group with more information than most. This can cause you some problems, since most people go to networking meetings to gain a new perspective about how to find a job and how and where to get more contacts. If you know a great deal about the process, you will be viewed as a "subject expert". When the word gets out, you will be highly sought after, so many will flock to you to get your opinion and elicit your help. This attention, although flattering, will thwart your efforts to gather the important information you need to move your job search forward. Don't run the risk of becoming a networking meeting junkie. Know the reason you want to join the group, look for a group that has a nice balance of people who are at a similar employment level as you are, and limit the number of groups you join so that you can put more effort into your own search.

Be cautious about the number of groups you join. Don't become a meeting junkie. Your primary focus needs to be your own job search. You can't afford to spend too much time supporting other's job search efforts.

How do I focus my energy on building a new pipeline?

Many job-seekers forget to tap into some great resources. Here is a list of some of my favorites:

- Family and friends – a trusted resource that is most likely to want to help you because they know and love you.

- Former supervisors and colleagues – this is another group that knows your work and could easily serve as a trusted, authentic resource for you.

- The Alumni Association and the Director of Alumni Relations from your university – this resource is often overlooked. Remember, your alumni association wants to keep you happy in the hope that you will grace the school with a donation. They are a wealth of information on who went to the same school and where they work.

- Professional Affiliations – this resource allows you to rub elbows with people who are working in an industry you want to work in, and they often know where the jobs are.

What is the appropriate way to connect with others to form new networking contacts?

There are wonderful organizations that can help you connect with others to for networking groups, and you can use services such as Meetingwave.com or Meetup.com. Check the availability of job search teams at your local out-placement firms, or look for the nearest Waggle Force Job Club. Some organizations offer opportunities such as "pink slip" parties where job-seekers and recruiters can mingle and talk about new career options.

You can also start your own job club. Many coffee shops and restaurants have job-seekers in their facilities. People who are out of work, often try to get out of their houses to break up the monotony of being home alone. You can usually spot people who are alone at a restaurant working on their laptops. Don't be a stalker, but do start a conversation. You may find that they would love the opportunity to do some networking with you.

Should I use a blast email to let people know I am available?

This is a practice that I highly disagree with. You are not, and should not be spam! As we have seen from all of the business and social websites, people are vastly more connected than ever before. Why would you risk the negative image that can be produced by blasting your documents out all over the place? A professional should always act as such. What you will most likely attract from your email blast is all of the "barracudas" out there that will happily offer you positions that are not real. They will offer you "jobs" that require you to pay a deposit. You also run the risk of having your personal information stolen. An email blast opens you up for all sorts of problems.

The most effective way to find a new position is to network well and to try to get yourself in front of as many hiring managers as possible.

How can I best make my network work for me?

Networking to get your next job is one of the most powerful tools you can use. Many people, however, are so afraid of the process that they avoid opportunities to accelerate their job search. You can shave months off your job search simply by getting out of your house and meeting people in person. Not so scary, yet many people feel networking is another form of begging. Once you have changed your mindset, you can use the variety of networks you have to effectively set your job search in motion.

Let's first talk about the types of networks you have:

- Social – family and friends

- Religious –connections from your church, temple or mosque

- Employment – former colleagues including supervisors.

- Second Degree – friends of friends, parents of your children's friends, etc.

- Volunteer Associates – people you meet through volunteer or community service you do.

- Future Associates – people you seek out for the purpose of networking, i.e. LinkedIn® connections through researching companies you could appropriately work for.

How can you make these networks work for you?

First, you need to make a commitment to tap into each and every network you have. Rotate the order of use, but definitely use each and every network.

I believe that being authentic is the most important thing you can be. Know that you have the power to get a job on your own, but that other people can often give us great ideas that put us on the right track for finding that job faster. I like it when you approach people in your network by saying: *"I am in a full blown job search, but I am not looking for you to find me a job. I know that you know many people. I am looking for an opportunity in (name an industry) and I was wondering if you can think of someone I should be talking with?"*

Avoid giving your network contacts jobs to do for you. Even if they are kind enough to tell you they will pass your resume on to someone else, thank them for being willing to do so, and tell them that you do not want them to feel they are your recruiter, so you would be happy to do all of the follow-up with the contact, if they would share the contact information with you.

If you simply commit to making five contacts every day, you will be amazed at how quickly ideas and opportunities will come up for you that will lead to your next position.

Another way to demystify networking is to remember that if you are the type of person who loves helping others, you are not alone. Let those in your network benefit from helping you. Be clear by telling them how they can help you, and you should take the responsibility to follow up with them. Again, try not to give them lots of jobs to do for you.

How can I reinvigorate my network when I feel it is drying up?

When you first start to network with others, it is easy to be excited and energized, but as time passes it is common for people to feel that their network is drying up. Don't despair because there are many hidden gems that can invigorate your network. Organizations such as your alumni office, professional affiliate groups and local networking clubs can be great sources of new information. You can also increase the number of target organizations you have by doing a premium database search that increases the radius of your search by at least five miles.

If you have children, begin to go to their soccer, baseball or football games so that you can network with other parents. Another great source for networking is by doing some volunteer work. It is a great place to meet new people and you are giving back to the community at the same time.

What kind of voice message should you leave to entice people to return your call?

The concept of leaving a message is interesting because the one thing a job-seeker never wants to be viewed as is what I refer to as a "stalker". When you are anxiously awaiting an answer from anyone: a hiring manager, a Human Resources professional, a networking contact, it is hard to resist calling the person often to make contact. You need to avoid being viewed as annoying, yet you want an answer that will help you find out where you stand in the job search process. There are several possible solutions to this dilemma.

First, you can satisfy your need to be a "stalker" by simply calling the person, and not leaving a message. Keep calling until you get the person directly. Most times the person will not know it was you, so you can call to your heart's content. When you leave a message, you must wait at least five days before you follow up with a second call. This process can be very tedious to the job-seeker.

If you are calling a former contact, you need to first clarify in your own mind the purpose of the call. The initial call should simply be a follow up to touch base with the person. You should not be asking that person to help you find a job. Most people do not feel they have the power to find you a position, and by asking for help you are taking an unfair advantage of the situation.

Renew your former relationship and authentically work to find out how the person has been. Be sure to set up a future time to have a great industry conversation, but don't ask for help. It is permissible to ask for a new network connection, but you should not ask for a job.

12

LinkedIn®

"Don't bend; don't water it down; don't try to make it logical;
don't edit your own soul according to the fashion.
Rather, follow your most intense obsessions mercilessly."

— Franz Kafka

LinkedIn® (www.LinkedIn.com) is a business networking site. It is a fabulous resource for the job-seeker. It was started in 1993 by the founders of PayPal®, and at this writing in 2012, its integrity has been preserved. Most people use it appropriately. By that I mean, they do not send out blast emails to promote their new businesses. It is a powerful source for networking. Remember, your next job will most likely come from networking!

Some of the most popular ways to use LinkedIn® are:

1. To build up your network.

2. To search for connections you already have in a particular organization that you are targeting.

3. To set up job alerts.

4. To keep track of what the people in your network are doing professionally.

5.   To prepare for an interview by learning more about the people in an organization.

6.   To join affiliate groups that are composed of like-minded people and who may be aware of new industry opportunities for you.

Should I use LinkedIn®?

I am a fan of the LinkedIn® site. I think that it gives the job-seeker easy access to all of the people in their network who could potentially help them accelerate their search. I also feel that as long as it remains true to its original purpose, it will be a great resource and I highly recommend taking a class or teleseminar so that you can use this service well.

LinkedIn® offers you the opportunity to create a profile, add recommendations, search for people and organizations, join groups and look for jobs.

One of the features I especially love is the area on your LinkedIn® account where you can post what you are doing. As soon as you post something new, that update goes out to all your connections. It is a great way to stay on someone's radar screen.

What are the benefits to upgrade my LinkedIn® account?

LinkedIn® allows, for a fee, additional service that will increase your ability to send direct "Inmails" (LinkedIn's terminology for email) to people. It facilitates introductions between you and the 2nd and 3rd level generation network contacts. My caution is that since there is no definite time table for how soon you will land your new position, so while you are out of work, you might want to be frugal and not spend additional money that you may need for more critical expenses.

What are the benefits of having recommendations on my LinkedIn® account?

LinkedIn® is a powerful networking tool. Many Hiring Managers comb through LinkedIn® accounts to see what a prospective employee posts about himself/herself. They also pay close attention to what others have said about you. In this age of confidentially laws, most of the larger organizations will not allow supervisors to give recommendations on former employees. At best, the Human Resource Department will only provide a potential employer with your most recent title and the total number of years you were employed by the organization.

This is a sad state of affairs for the job-seeker, since your potential new employer would love to be able to talk directly with someone for whom you had worked, in order to better assess your competence as an employee. This is a situation where LinkedIn® can be very helpful. By asking former supervisors and colleagues to post an endorsement of your work on LinkedIn®, they can speak on your behalf, yet not serve as the mouthpiece for your former company. It is a simple solution to the problem of collecting recommendations from those who know your work, yet are bound by their organizations not to give official recommendations out on former employees.

Another benefit from using LinkedIn® is that every time you change something in your profile, it alerts everyone in your network. It is a great way to stay on everyone's radar.

Should I post my photo on LinkedIn®?

My rule of thumb is that job-seekers should not post photos until after they have landed a new job. Although some would disagree, I maintain that whether we admit to it or even recognize what we are doing, most of us form instant opinions, even stereotypes from the reaction we have to a photo. A hiring manager may unknowingly react to your gender, race, age or any number of factors subconsciously, and, that very reaction will keep them from calling you in for an interview.

As a job-seeker, your primary goal is to land an interview. You do not need any distractions that will hurt your chances of getting that all-important interview!

Certainly, once you have landed a job, including a professional photo on your LinkedIn® account is a great idea. People do like memory triggers so a photo is a great way to remind people of who you are professionally.

Remember: No job, no photo!

Is there a limit to the number of LinkedIn® groups I should join?

What are the benefits to joining LinkedIn® groups? There is a limit to all forms of networking if it gets in the way of your productivity with regard to your job search. You should ask yourself why you feel you need to belong to so many groups. Networking is not the pursuit of a social life. It is unlikely that you will need more than three groups to satisfy all of your networking needs.

Choose well and remember to balance the time you spend engaging in group activities with other essential activities that will support your job search.

How should I structure a subject line and email through LinkedIn® if I do not know the person, but want to connect?

The subject lines that never works are: "Looking for a job," or "I need help". I think you need to be more subtle and start off with something like: "Looking for some information" or "Collecting data". You should be very clear about the purpose of your email. Don't ambush the person by asking them to help you get into their company. Start by telling them you are collecting data on their company or industry and would like to have a conversation with them. Most people who do not know us would be reluctant to offer much help, but LinkedIn® is often a wonderful vehicle for getting introduced to the right people in your target company.

Should you update your LinkedIn® profile where your former organization is listed as "present" or leave it there to give the appearance that you are still employed?

I always feel you need to take the high road. Just be honest. Put the year you left your job and walk with your head held high. You won't make a very good impression on the Hiring Manager if it looks like you aren't authentic.

What are the criteria for accepting a LinkedIn® request?

I think that you should always accept an invitation from someone you know and admire. The difficulty comes in when you receive a request from someone you do not know. In that case, do as much research as possible to find out about them. Check out their network of connections carefully. If there are no glaring reasons to ignore the invitation, then, by all means, accept it.

Remember, LinkedIn®'s purpose is to help you network on a grand scale. I do think, however, that if you are sent an invitation by someone you know, but the person does not share your values or integrity, you should not link to them. Your association with that person may be viewed unfavorably, so don't run the risk of being linked to someone with whom you would be embarrassed to be associated.

13

Transition
What's Age Got To Do With It?

"Failure is a prerequisite to success.
Our biggest failures become our greatest teachers;
the lessons we learn become the foundation of success."

— Marcia Wieder

This chapter is being written by special request from one of my clients who felt that I should address the issue of what comes next if you are fifty plus in age and you have been laid off.

I think there are some mixed messages out there. If you listen to the news, you will surely believe that no one over fifty will get another job. You're done! You might as well start your own business because you are completely unmarkctable!

And then you meet people like me, who truly believe that you can be marketable at any age if you do certain things to ensure that you are truly marketable.

Step One to being marketable at any age, is to look current with regard to your hair, make up and clothing. First and foremost, take a hard look at your looks! If you are still wearing clothes from your closet that date back to the 1950's or 70's, or 80's...you get the picture. I know they are still in good shape, but get rid of them! You only get three seconds to make a good impression, and what does it say about you as a potential candidate if you look like you are living the past?

And what's with that hairdo and hair color? I totally believe that authenticity is the key to success, but authenticity comes from within. It does not mean you have to take a passive approach to how you look. Get a makeover, get a new do (this goes for men, as well) and find a fashionista or an image consultant who will help you look your best in today's modern world.

Step Two is to pull yourself up by the boot straps, and go get some new education. If you haven't stepped foot in a classroom since 1975, you are due, and I might add, you will be amazed at how much easier and more pleasant it is to go to school as an adult than it ever was when you were eighteen! If you are not interested in matriculating in a new college degree program, at least take some classes relevant to your industry, or in this age of personal development, do some inner work to help you discover your purpose and open your mind to gratitude and possibilities. Education is the thing that gets you unstuck. Employers love to hire employees who are confident and secure, not those who are angry and dejected. Education and open-mindedness really help you to be confident. Taking classes also open up your world to new contacts and the sharing of ideas.

A kissing cousin to education, in the staying marketable game, is to know your industry, which is **Step Three**. Whether you are currently working or not, take some time every day to read industry journals and newspapers. The more you know about your industry, the more attractive you will be to a Hiring Manager. When a position comes up, so will your name if you have had great industry conversations with people in the power to hire you.

Step Four is to beef up your technology skills. There is nothing that screams ageism more than a lack of technology skills. I know, everyone born after 1976 was born with technology in their veins! There wasn't a time in their lives that there wasn't technology. They seem to be able to learn everything with such ease.

Well, here's a newsflash, the computer age is here to stay. It is up to you to find someone you can understand, and have them teach all you need to know to keep up with everyone in the workplace whether they are 20 or 60; you just can't lag behind! Check out your public library for basic classes and your local community college for more advanced non-credit classes. Don't get left behind simply because you haven't kept your skills up.

Step Five is always have a Can-do attitude. It seems like this one is obvious, but many people who have been laid off send out very negative vibes without being aware of it.

Attitude is something we can't hide. It comes through loud and clear. It is truly disappointing to lose a job, at any age, but know that there are more jobs out there and the sooner you realize that in every difficult situation there is a gift, the sooner you will move forward toward that next opportunity.

Spend some quiet time reflecting on the gift your new freedom will bring you. Stop being angry and start planning your next steps so that you can get into action and keep your job search active and exciting.

At the end of the day, we need to take a difficult situation, like losing a job and turn it into the gift of action, adventure and fun. Looking for a job should consist of using current, tried and true career development techniques, coupled with the sense of adventure to find and connect with an organization that is a great fit for your skills, education, personality, and financial needs.

It is like searching for that next love affair... it's out there, and there is nothing more satisfying than to have someone love you for who you are... it's true in life and it's true in work. We need to go on the journey, filled with ups and downs, in order to find the person or organization who gets us, and, more importantly, wants us because we are right for them. When you find an organization that wants to hire you, it is just like being in love. I can hear Sally Fields shouting: "You like me, you really,

really like me!" There is nothing more gratifying than to hear a Hiring Manager say they would be delighted to have you join their organization!

All of this being said, finding that job takes a long time. That has very little to do with your age. Remember that if your resume is written carefully, there should be no "red flags" regarding age on it. Although you know how old you are, those reading your resume should not. If you look good, are full of vitality and have lots of industry knowledge, you are a great candidate.

Some of the success in weathering the transitional period between one job and another lies in your ability to stay up beat as you do some serious networking. You are most likely to get a new job based on recommendations from those who have had direct contact with you.

Don't spend too much time on the job boards, especially if you are an executive. You probably have so many skills that there would not be a job large enough for you. Your vast experience will never show up as a job posting. You are already bigger than that.

Spend your days getting in front of people in the industry. One great way to do that is to attend industry affiliation meetings. Volunteer to serve on a committee so that others can evaluate your work.

Another option you have, if you are entrepreneurial, is to start your own business. If you have never owned your own business before, it would be of value for you to take advantage of the free classes that you can take through the SCORE Organization. Visit www.SCORE.org for a list of classes in your area. They will also assign a counselor to work with you at no cost to you.

Remember that all of the elements of running a great business are the same whether you are a solopreneur or you are part of a huge organization. Be sure you have all the elements covered, either by you or by a staff you hire. I am a huge proponent of getting a virtual staff. There are so many fabulous virtual assistants out there. Ask friends for recommendations.

Your virtual staff will be the support you need to make you successful. Be sure to ask what they specialize in. If you need someone who has marketing savvy, be sure you hire someone with that specialty. If you need a bookkeeper, do the same.

Don't be a micromanager, it doesn't matter where they live, and the only thing that matters is what they can do for your business that will support you in areas where you do not excel or areas you are too busy to focus on.

How do I know I have made the right decision/discerned to leave my career to go to a new one?

One of the best things you can do BEFORE leaving your current career is to do some research on the industry you are interested in moving into. What are the trends in that industry? Is it a sustainable industry that will be around for a long time? (Examples include: healthcare, education and technology — although the technology will change, if you are hard-wired to understand technology, you can survive in that industry.)

The next step is to find out what new education you will need to assure you are ready to move into that industry. It takes more than a simple desire to change from one industry to another. You need to have the current education specific to that industry. Don't try to skip this step because even if you get hired based on your good reputation in another industry, you will be constantly wondering what you were doing there! Be prepared before you move into that new industry!

Lastly, before you get the education and switch to the new industry, go on informational interviews with people in the new industry. Ask questions of those in the trenches of that industry. Everything looks better from the outside!

I will give you an example: I know a woman who decided that she wanted to become an airline stewardess. She signed up for the training and went through the entire program. She was finally ready and was assigned to go on her first trip as a stewardess. I spoke with her shortly after that first flight. To my surprise, she was ready to quit! When I asked her what had happened, she said that she never realized that she would feel like a waitress in the sky! She clearly didn't do the research beforehand!

If a position sounds like something you would be interested in, find someone who does that job and ask if you can speak with them. Get the information you will need to make your decision directly from someone doing the job.

What factors should I weigh before changing careers?

I have actually addressed some of the factors above so here's an overview:

- Research the sustainability of the new industry.

- Determine how much new education you will need to be successful in that industry.

- Have conversations with people doing the job you hope to do in the future.

- Do a little soul-searching to see if this new industry is in alignment with who you are as a person.

- See if you can shadow someone who is doing the job in the new industry you want to move in to. This can be a great way to really assess whether or not you would enjoy the position.

- Work with a coach to have them drill down with you to assess whether or not this move is for you. Don't ever make a move based on the state of your checkbook or on an emotional whim. There are wonderful coaches out there who are worth their weight in gold. They can help you determine whether or not a move is good for you. Yes, coaches cost money, but isn't it worth investing a couple of thousand dollars to help you land a six-figure job in an industry that matches your skills and needs?

- Some organizations will offer internship opportunities to people at any age. There may not be financial remuneration for the internship, but it will give you great experiential opportunities that will help you decide whether or not the industry/ job is right for you. In the end, it will also give you the hands-on experience that most employers want you to have if they are going to hire you.

14

Good Enough

"There is no traffic jam on the extra mile."

— Zig Zigler

Sadly, the one thing I seem to encounter in most of my clients, no matter how successful they have been prior to being laid off from a job, is their expression of concern about not being "good enough." That need for perfection seems to be universal and really rears its ugly head when someone has been derailed by the loss of a job, especially if they were doing well and loved that job. It saddens me to see fabulous employees, who have worked for years to move up the corporate ladder, beat themselves up and consequently put up road blocks to their job search.

As is truc with many of the ideas we get that block our progress, if we simply change the way we look at the concept, we can change the effect it has on us. I propose that a simple change in our mindset can occur through the use of different punctuation. For example, if a person feels that their work is not good enough, then by changing the punctuation, the two words can read: Good! Enough. Rather than the negative concept that you or your work is not good enough, wouldn't it be better if you believed that all that you did in your career was good and you have done enough, hence: *Good! Enough.*

Throughout this guide we have talked several times about mindset. We talked about how different you would feel if every time you went into an interview, you believed that the Hiring Manager not only thought that you were competent to do the job that they had available, but that they wanted YOU to be the one they hired. Your mindset would allow you to go into the interview full of the kind of confidence that Hiring Managers want in their employees.

We have also talked about your mindset with regard to the way you feel about getting laid off, and that the sooner you put any negative feelings aside, the sooner you will create opportunities to land a new position.

Your mindset is a powerful force in every aspect of your life. When negative, it can keep you blocked, which often makes the job search take a very long time. When positive, it can be the driving force to finding that next new, great job. If you find yourself in the state of negativity all the time, consider taking some courses in self-development.

There are many techniques that are easily learned and can help move you forward. Learning effective goal setting or how to create affirmations can lift your spirits and drive you forward. Other techniques include meditation, hypnosis or neurolinguistic programming. Each of these techniques tap into the subconscious mind and help release the negative blocks that are often the result of negative scripts you have been telling yourself for years.

One way to recognize whether or not you are stuck is to start paying attention to the questions you are asking yourself. If you constantly ask questions such as: "Why did this happen to me?" or "Why won't anyone hire me?" you keep yourself in the state of inertia. "Why" questions keep you stuck.

One very simple technique to get yourself unstuck is to start asking yourself "How" questions. "How can I use my network of family and friends to help me get a new job?" "How can I get directly in front of a Hiring Manager?" "How can I structure my resume to best reflect my ability to do the posted job at the company I choose?"

Paying attention to the things you say and the way you think about yourself has a profound effect on your job search and your life. Always keep focused on the fact that what you have done is "Good!" and it was, indeed, "Enough". Take yourself out of the negative spiral downward that a lack of self-worth can bring.

Start paying attention to the things people say about you. Listen to the compliments that people pay you and pay special attention to the thank you notes people send you. A thank you note is thanking you for that piece of yourself that you have generously given to another human being. Keep them and pull them out when you are feeling down. Remembering the person who wrote it and the event you shared together can lift your spirits. Good self-esteem comes from recognizing your innate talents and how you have successfully used them. Having good self-esteem can give you the confidence to move your job search forward.

If I take a "temp to hire position," what do I do about my resume and LinkedIn® profile?

This is a time where I do not feel it is necessary to change your documents immediately. You have a bit of time, and if you are continuing to look for a permanent position, it might be best to hold off until you are in a permanent position. The best example I can give you is that it is like having a job that requires a three month-probation. You have the job, but it isn't permanent until you have passed the probation period. In this case, you can wait to change your profile until you have a permanent job.

What will the next employer think if I take a "stop gap" position?

A simple answer is the employer will think you were protecting yourself and your family. When the economy is bad, and thousands of people are out of work, the playing field has changed. Hiring Managers know that there is job scarcity and that it is not uncommon for a person to take a short-term position in order to survive, even if it is a lower position.

The other thing to consider is that there isn't too much of a gap in your work history, and if you just recently started the new position, you do not need to mention it. You can see how things play out. Just remember that if you do take a new position shortly after taking a stop-gap position, you still would be required to give the proper notice if you need to leave that position.

How do I avoid jumping at the first job that comes along, especially if it is at a lower level than my previous job?

This is a sensitive question because it often hinges on your finances. If you have been laid off and have received a good severance package and if you have always been frugal with your money, you may have the luxury of time and can continue your search without feeling the need to jump at the first job that comes to you. I don't, however, recommend throwing caution to the wind. Be realistic about your finances and if you have a safety net, take the time to weigh all your options and look for a position that is at or above the level of the position you just left. If your finances are in order, you can engage in a job search for the most appropriate job, or better yet, you can have the luxury of looking at what it would take to get into the job of your dreams. If you always plan ahead, you will have the luxury of avoiding the "desperation job."

Praise for Angela Schutz and
Ask *Angela*

"*Angela is truly working within her passion as a career coach. She is patient, knowledgeable and very gifted in her skills, including bringing out the best in others. She has the gift of seeing only potential and opportunity at every turn, and helps others believe in themselves and what they can accomplish. She uses a very non-judgmental approach to helping those of us who need a nudge, a boost, or a smack upside the head to get moving in our search. Angela guides inspires and motivates the people and teams with whom she works to reach their full potential. She sees beyond the limits that people have imposed on themselves to get them to reach beyond their comfort zone and strive for the excellence they can achieve. I highly recommend Angela to anyone who needs someone in their corner when trying to assess their skills and talents in today's ever changing job search marketplace.*"

- Kelly W.

"*Angela has a masterful way of coaching you to achieve your dreams, not to just find a job. Her breadth of professional knowledge and passion for helping others enables her to take your initial fear and self-doubt and turn it into renewed self-confidence.*"

- Gina A.

Praise for Angela Schutz and Ask Angela

"I met Angela at a time when I was professionally bereft. Thanks to Angela's intuition, motivation, compassion and her fortitude in keeping me moving forward and not looking back, I went back to school and started a new career. Angela's help has spilled into all areas of my life. I consider myself blessed to have met Angela."

- Carol D.

"Angela is a consummate professional with the highest degree of integrity, honesty and customer service. Angela is extremely passionate in her role as a career coach and is constantly striving to assist her clients in going above and beyond. Angela is one of the most knowledgeable professionals within her field and is always able to find and bring out the best in every client she engages. Her perception and persistence helped her many clients not just to succeed, but to exceed their goals and expectations

I highly recommend Angela to any person or corporation looking to provide industry leading skills, ability and insight in improving their career prospects, goals and achievements."

- Robert L.

"Packed with innovative ideas to get you on the right path, here is the easy-to-follow guide that will take the stress out of your job search. This is a no-nonsense approach toward landing your next position. I have trained Angela and whether she is serving as a Certified Dream Coach or Career Coach, she has a huge heart but is no push over."

- MarciaWieder
CEO/Founder Dream University®

"I am pleased to provide my recommendation for Angela Schutz. Angela is a seasoned Career Coach and provides her vast knowledge of the job market and human resources for the benefit of her clients. She keeps her clients on task and challenges them to use every venue and method possible to achieve their goals. She is also extremely personable and would be an asset to any organization."

- Robert D.

~ A Special Gift ~

Thank you for purchasing this book. I truly hope you enjoyed it and are more motivated to transform your career. As my way of thanking you, I would like to send you a gift. If you send me your receipt for the purchase of this book, I will send you a complimentary copy of my new cd of jokes entitled: ***Ask Angela: How to Live Life Laughing.***

It is just a little something to brighten your day as you continue to search for that perfect new job. Send your original receipt plus your mailing address to:

Ask Angela's Free CD Offer
C/O Driven to Succeed Consulting LLC
554 Boston Post Road, Suite 171
Orange, CT 06477

About The Author

Angela I. Schutz, M.A.

I have decided that bios can be pretty boring and I really don't want to do that to you. Mostly what I think you need to know about me is that I can relate to you, the job-seeker because I have been there. I have felt the pain of losing a job I loved – three times!

Yes, over the course of my lifetime, I have lost three jobs, all of which I truly loved and would never have left, if given the choice, but what I found out is that each and every time I lost a job, something new emerged in an unusual way and each new job, although often extremely different from the previous one, stretched me in wonderful ways and caused me to grow into a more flexible, more creative and better equipped employee. Each job gave me the opportunity to develop new skills that I had no idea I had. Over time, I came to realize that the most important trait one can have is that of being open-minded. Learning so many new skills brought with it a modicum of confidence that wasn't there before. The process helped me fully step into who I was meant to be. So to each of the bosses who told me my time was up at their company, thank you. I will forever be indebted to you for giving me the wings to grow!

For those of you for whom curiosity is a major trait and for others who are dying to know who fired me, here is my traditional and somewhat stuffy bio so that you can solve the mystery! Have at it, if you must, or set it aside and simply know, I have been propelled since I was very young to explore who I am and what I do best. It has been quite a journey since I have worked in at least three industries and have held many, many titles, some loftier than others, but I can safely tell you that the one true thing about me is that I am always professionally passionate! I love my work, no matter what it is and I love exploring new options, so if you are a Hiring Manager – let's talk because I am still open to the exploration of new employment opportunities!

And for those who want specifics ...

Angela I. Schutz is the Managing Director and Founder of Driven to Succeed Consulting LLC, a career development and executive coaching service aimed at empowering people to find their ultimate career potential. She has also served as a University Relations Career Consultant and a Certified Associate for Lee Hecht Harrison, an international career management organization ranked second in out placement services. Angela served as a career consultant to hundreds of clients in search and to students earning their MBA and EMBA degrees.

Angela has served as the Executive Director of Training and Development for the National Society of Leadership and Success. In this capacity her duties included serving as the online success coach for undergraduate students across the country who were members of this national honor society. She served as the primary support person for chapter advisors and student chapter presidents. Her duties extended to areas of sales, marketing and publicity.

While employed by the University of New Haven, Angela served as the Director of Career Services and Experiential Learning. In this capacity, she was responsible for directing the Career Development Office and building external relations with individuals and companies that contributed to the future growth of the university and provided employment opportunities for students. She was also a key player in the launching a new experiential learning program that would support and enhance the university's commitment to "real-life learning" by partnering with major corporations to offer both scholarship and internship opportunities to students. During her time at the UNH, Angela held several other key positions. She has served as the Program Director for the Program to China. Through her travels to China and her ability to work closely with other cultures, Angela has facilitated educational programs for students from China as they worked to receive their master degrees and bridge cultural gaps. She created a specialized program in architecture for architects from China.

Angela served as the Assistant Dean for Academic Services. In this capacity, she created a streamlined advising process for first-year students which employed an "active" advising approach that encouraged faculty advisors to use academic and campus resources to their fullest.

Angela received her academic education at Gateway Community College where she earned her Associates Degree and Southern Connecticut State University where she earned her Bachelor of Arts in Psychology. She completed her graduate work at the University of New Haven earning a Master of Arts in Community Psychology.

Angela exhibits a true love of learning and strives to mentor students through her professional passion. She is a qualified Myers-Briggs Type Indicator Administrator and holds a Management Certificate in Higher Education from the Higher Education Resource Service (HERS) from Wellesley College.

In 2009, Angela was chosen as one of one hundred individuals from around the world to take part in the Train the Trainer program with the author, Jack Canfield (Chicken Soup for the Soul® series and The Success Principles). She is certified to teach success empowerment workshops. She is also a professional speaker and speaks on topics that span all phases of career development as well as success empowerment. She holds five Career Consultation certifications. She has facilitated career learning sessions for such organizations as Women for Hire. In 2010, she was chosen to be in the Spark and Hustle program for entrepreneurial women and was mentored by Tory Johnson, Founder and CEO of Women for Hire. She is a certified Dream Coach through Dream Coach University® founded by Marcia Wieder and has studied Neuro-

Linguistic Programming with Sean Smith. She is an adjunct professor at Gateway Community College.

Angela is a member of the Foundation Board for Gateway Community College in New Haven, Connecticut. She is also a member of the University of New Haven Alumni Association, where she previously held consecutive executive offices for seven years. She is on the Professional Development Committee for the Eastern Association of Colleges and Employers and is an active member of the Association of Psychological Type and the Association of Coaching Professionals International. Her volunteer work includes teaching for Junior Achievement and volunteering for the American Cancer Society. She is committed to the education of college students and serves as an adjunct professor. She has also established a scholarship in memory of her mother at Gateway Community College. She resides in Connecticut. To connect with Angela, visit her website at www.driventosucceed.net.

Index

www.ingramcontent.com/pod-product-compliance
Lightning Source LLC
Chambersburg PA
CBHW030842210326
41521CB00025B/822